You Give Me the Sun

After you finish reading *You Give Me the Sun,* you may want to read these other books for teens from Saint Mary's Press:

The Catholic Youth Bible

This first-of-its-kind, NEW Bible helps you
- answer life's important questions
- see yourself as a vital part of God's saving work in the world
- make connections to Catholic beliefs and traditions
- read the Bible regularly
- *study* the Bible, *pray* the Bible, *live* the Bible

In addition to the complete Bible text, *The Catholic Youth Bible* contains over 650 lively articles. These insightful articles address your questions about God and your everyday concerns. This unique Bible is for you!

Good News, Day by Day: Bible Reflections for Teens

These 365 reflections offer you the Good News each day of the year. Short reflections after each passage show you how to live the way God wants you to, and short prayers invite you to pray with the Bible. Its handy size makes this book perfect for your pocket, your backpack, or your bedside.

Stations for Teens:
Meditations on the Death and Resurrection of Jesus Christ

This book contains meditations on the fourteen stations of the cross. It introduces twelve Scripture stories as stations of the Resurrection. And most important, it sheds light on the struggle to believe that sin and death have been conquered, that Jesus has been raised, and that the Holy Spirit is with us today.

Prayers Before an Awesome God: The Psalms for Teenagers

The author, David Haas, brings the Psalms to life in *Prayers Before an Awesome God: The Psalms for Teenagers.* This book will help you give meaningful expression to your varied life experiences, for in the Psalms we find ways to express joy and sadness, excitement and loneliness, peace and rage.

To order, visit your local bookstore or call Saint Mary's Press at 800-533-8095.

You Give Me the Sun

Biblical Prayers by Teenagers

Edited by Carl Koch

Saint Mary's Press
Christian Brothers Publications
Winona, Minnesota

The publishing team included Carl Koch,
development editor; Laurie A. Berg, copy
editor; James H. Gurley, production editor;
Hollace Storkel, typesetter; Cären Yang,
designer; Cindi Ramm, art director; Erica
Rose Krauthamer, cover illustration; pre-
press, printing, and binding by the graphics
division of Saint Mary's Press.

Printed in the United States of America

Printing: 9 8 7 6 5 4 3 2 1

Year: 2008 07 06 05 04 03 02 01 00

ISBN 0-88489-615-3

Genuine recycled paper with 10% post-
consumer waste.
Printed with soy-based ink.

Contents

Preface 7

Thanks 9

Personal Matters 34

Friends and Family 59

The Big Picture 65

Talking with God 91

Index by School 111

Preface

In 1991 Saint Mary's Press published *Dreams Alive: Prayers by Teenagers.* Because of the enthusiastic response to that book, we asked teenagers to send us prayers for *More Dreams Alive,* which came out in 1995. Again, the response to this new book of prayers by teenagers was overwhelmingly positive.

As part of the mission of Saint Mary's Press to spread the Good News by encouraging people to pray with the Scriptures, we decided to ask teenagers to send us their prayers and reflections based on favorite passages from the Bible. *You Give Me the Sun* is the result.

Each prayer in the book includes one quoted line from the Bible around which the prayer is written. The topics the teens choose to write about range from the humorous to the most serious. In all cases the prayers reflect honesty, authenticity, and an awareness of the real world of high-school-age people.

When teachers or catechists selected prayers for submission, the writers were given the opportunity to attach their full name, their initials, their first name, or to remain anonymous. All the prayers are identified by the school or parish from which they came.

Prayers and reflections poured in from all over: Massachusetts to Puerto Rico, Washington to Alabama. As with the previous two books of teen prayers, the sheer number, quality, and diversity dazzled me.

After an initial reading, sorting, and selecting, I asked six students to help with the final selection: Tim Singer-Towns and Beth Angst from Cotter High School; and Ryan Hinton, Alodia Verhage, Jackie Paul, and Matt Palkert from Saint Mary's University of Minnesota, both located in Winona, Minnesota. The contribution of this team of students was indispensable and is greatly appreciated.

Using the Prayers

The prayers and reflections in this book are useful to teenagers individually, as well as in ministry settings and family gatherings. Following are some suggestions for their use:

Teenagers and adults who work in ministry settings—such as campus ministry—might consider using the prayers in these ways:
- to start or end a class
- to give focus to a prayer session
- as part of a retreat
- to trigger discussion about topics of importance to teens
- as part of a parent, sponsor, or staff meeting

This book would be a helpful gift to parents and to adults who work with teens in secular settings. The prayers can remind adults that teenagers are people of faith. Teenagers have a unique and lively perspective on faith, the world, relationships, and themselves.

The uses of *You Give Me the Sun* are limited only by one's creativity. If you find a unique way to use this book, we would love to hear about it. Write to us at Saint Mary's Press, 702 Terrace Heights, Winona, MN 55987-1320, or e-mail us at *www.smp.org*.

A Final Word of Thanks

A book like this would not be possible without the contributions and cooperation of many people:
- Thanks to the diocesan, parish, and school personnel who got the word out, gathered and submitted the prayers.
- Thanks to the parents, teachers, and catechists who nurture the faith of teenagers in families, schools, and parishes.
- Thanks to all the students who allowed their prayers and reflections to be submitted for consideration. I only wish that we could have published all of them.

You Give Me the Sun is a gift of teenagers to all of us. My wish is that every person who opens this book finds in it consolation, inspiration, and great hope.

Carl Koch
Editor

Thanks

I led them with cords of human kindness,
with bands of love.
(Hosea 11:4)

A quiet place where distractions are not
allowed is a perfect place to be.
When alone with Christ, I pray for
peace and victory.

A quiet time I sit and watch the
sun rise, as I watch the sweet days of
autumn swiftly pass by. The world is
soft and settled. There is still
time to hush my words.

Oh, Lord, make the moments count!
We have one life to live, so
guide us by your Holy Word.
Today's the day to give!

In a quiet place, I wonder if
love could ever be a golden rope that
links me to my mother's heart.
In a quiet place, I know that there is a
special feeling in my
father's touch; his strength is secure.
With all this love through this
golden rope, this is what helps me to endure.

Shantell C. Griffin
West Philadelphia Catholic High School
Philadelphia, PA

Running with my Savior,
"they shall run and not be weary,
they shall walk and not faint" (Isaiah 40:31).

I saw them running past my street
not yielding to the tremendous heat

at first I thought it was just a joke
or maybe just an elaborate hoax

but as the endless pack jogged by
I wanted to get up and join their cry

they have been running for a real long time
running to taste the fruit of the vine

the man they follow is winning the race
he runs at a most frightening pace

he leads the way for his people to go
but it is up to them to join the show

but joining is not the most important part
instead it is acting from the heart

and if you finish the race in stride
you will receive a hefty prize

Tim Trainor
Elder High School
Cincinnati, OH

Give thanks to the LORD, for he is good.
(Psalm 106:1)

In the winter, the trees are asleep,
Ghosts of their former selves.

And the snow falls and softly
Blankets them with white.

And I thank you, God, for the
Quiet beauty of winter.

In the spring, the trees awaken
And shake off their white winter blanket.
New leaves appear,
And the winter, black and white,
Dissolves into the bright, cheerful noise
Of spring.

And I thank you, God, for the
New, emerging beauty of spring.

In the summer, the trees
Reach their leaves to the sky in praise.
They sway in gentle breezes
And shade the ground in shadows.

And I thank you, God, for the
Sparkling, sunlit beauty of summer.

In the autumn, the trees turn
Bright yellow and orange and scarlet.
The leaves say their good-byes in
Seas of color, then
Blanket the ground like the snow to come.

And I thank you, God, for the
Brilliant beauty of fall.

For all the seasons and all the days,
I thank you, God, in so many ways.

Sarah Cannon
Saint Gertrude High School
Richmond, VA

Sing to the LORD, for he has triumphed gloriously;
horse and rider he has thrown into the sea.

(Exodus 15:21)

Thank you, God my creator, for giving me life.
Thank you, God my mother, for protecting me from harm.
Thank you, God my hope and strength, you give me new beginnings.
Thank you, God my provider, for giving me all that I need.
Thank you, God my father, for doing what's best for me.
Thank you, God my creator, mother, father, strength, hope, confessor,
    and steadfast provider,
Thank you a thousand times!
And may I go to sleep each night grateful,
and each day begin with this prayer of thanks to you.

Mary-Frances Auner
Saint Augustine Academy
Lakewood, OH

Listen.
"SHH!"
Do not speak.
Do not breathe.
Do not move.
Listen carefully.

Do you hear?
Jesus is calling out to us in a whisper,
"Listen . . . and come to me;
listen, so that you may live" (Isaiah 55:2–3).

Listen carefully to the message of Jesus.
Jesus speaks.
Through a smile of a baby,
A laugh of a child,
A tear from a mother's eye,
A sigh of a father.

Through a thunderstorm that rips through the night,
A beautiful rose on a gravestone,
Jesus speaks.
Look around and you may find
Clues that show God is near.
Then you will know you have nothing to fear.

Alexis Diana Marie Christiansen
Saint Thomas More Academy
Magnolia, DE

Thanks for all the times you've helped when I've been in pain,
Thanks for all the times you've forgiven me when I used your name in
    vain.
Thanks for all the comfort you've given me when I'm feeling blue,
but if I could sit across the porch from God,
I'd thank him most for lending me you.
Thank you for hearing my prayer,
thanks for putting up with me when I'm in your hair.
"The borrower is the slave of the lender" (Proverbs 22:7).
So I am but a servant to you, Jesus, because you gave me your life.

C. B.
Bishop Manogue Catholic High School
Reno, NV

Jesus said, "You shall love your neighbor as yourself" (Matthew 22:39).
A couple of days ago, I lived this statement. I was at the mall, and
right when I came in, a man was sitting in a wheelchair. He was all by
himself and looked lonely, so I smiled at him. He smiled back at me as if
no one had ever smiled at him before. Although it wasn't a big action, I
could see that I made a difference in that one moment in his life, which
made me feel very good. Smiles go a long way.

Laura Leviski
Our Lady of Perpetual Help
Ellicott City, MD

O, give thanks to the LORD.

(Psalm 136:1)

My mom is the greatest
She cares for me and she's smart
But I wouldn't even know her if it weren't for you
So thank you from the bottom of my heart

My dad's a great motivator
Sometimes my brother is a pest
But when it comes right down to it
My family is the best

My friends are always there for me
Day, afternoon, and night
And we always pull through it
If we get in a fight

There's a roof over my head
Clothes on my back
Food in my stomach
And so much love, it's hard to keep track

And God . . .
You've helped me through when times were tough
And I could sit here and thank you a million times
And that still wouldn't be enough.

Katherine Wieland
Bishop Manogue Catholic High School
Reno, NV

I thank you, God our creator, for this day and for all the precious gifts with which you have blessed me. I thank you for the many talents you have given me, and ask that you give me the strength and the wisdom to use those gifts and talents to glorify you in the best way that I am able.

I ask that you hold close to your heart all those in tough situations. Whether they are in an abusive situation or a situation of pressure from friends and family, I ask that you keep them close to your heart. I ask also that you help teenagers understand that you are there for them as much as for anyone else. I think that sometimes, God, teenagers get the feeling that you only love those who are perfect or those who are older, but I ask of you today that you show them your unconditional love and forgiveness that they may become closer to you. I ask this in your name: teach them to realize that through you we "can do all things" (Philippians 4:13). Amen.

Gretchen Schmaltz
Roncalli High School
Indianapolis, IN

The Bible says: "The time came for her [Mary] to deliver her child. And she gave birth to her firstborn son and wrapped him in bands of cloth, and laid him in a manger" (Luke 2:6–7). This happened on Christmas day. Most people forget that this is the true meaning of the holiday. It isn't about getting presents or candy. Those things are great, but Jesus' birth is a million times greater. So come Christmastime, we ought to remember the true meaning of the special holiday. I know that I won't forget.

Chris Hildreth
Our Lady of Perpetual Help
Ellicott City, MD

The cup of blessing that we bless, is it not a sharing in the blood of Christ? The bread that we break, is it not a sharing in the body of Christ?

(1 Corinthians 10:16)

Dear God,
Thank you for the love I have with others.
For whatever we do, we are sharing in your love for others.
Thank you for your sacrifice, so that we can continue to carry on
 as you intended.
Thank you for your love, that burns so bright, that shines over me
 and guides me with your light.
Blessed are my foes; I do not think of them in spite, but rather do
 I fight to guide them to their light.
As I look upon my life, I know that I've done wrong,
 but I will pray that I'll always hear the sweetness of your song.
My thanks. Amen.

Ben Zyons
Bishop Hendricken High School
Warwick, RI

Every day of every week,
My guardian angel stands by my side.
Watching and listening to my every motion and my every sound,
She stands there protecting me.

On days when I'm feeling like I can't talk to anyone, she listens.
On days when I'm feeling like I don't know what to do,
She advises me in a way that I'm not really aware of.

No matter rain, shine, snow, or sleet,
She is always by my side,
Making sure the world is safe for me to walk around in,
Coming to help me whenever I need her.

I am thankful for her always being there
When I could only depend on her because no one else cared.
I am thankful to her for being the constant protector
Of my mind, body, and soul.

"For [God] will command his angels concerning you
to guard you in all your ways" (Psalm 91:11).

Sarah Binger
Bishop Manogue Catholic High School
Reno, NV

I call heaven and earth to witness against you today that I have set
before you life and death, blessings and curses. Choose life so that you
and your descendants may live.
(Deuteronomy 30:19)

To gaze upon the stars of night
To smell the sweet scent of pale pink roses
To feel the morning dew upon your fingertips
To hear the wind blow through rustling leaves
To taste cool, crisp water on your parched tongue
To sing
To dance
To smile
To eat
To laugh
To read
To pray
To love
To live.

These are things we often take for granted. Jesus, thank you for
the precious gift of life. Thank you for each step we take. Thank you
for each morning we awake. Thank you for our parents who chose life.
Thank you for each breath we take. We ask you, Creator God, to make
us instruments of your love and stand up for life.

C. L. C.
McGill-Toolen High School
Mobile, AL

Surely everyone stands as a mere breath.
　Surely everyone goes about like a shadow.
                                    (Psalm 39:5–6)

But God, never let me underestimate a breath.
Both life and death start with breath.
It can be felt as the soft whisper of a child against the ear,
Or as soothing breath on the sting of a cut.
It can carry impassioned cries or sweet lullabies.
It can be suspended and cut into mournful staccato.
A breath can be full of laughter, or regret, or relief.
God, with each breath help me remember
the transient beauty of life.

Jean Gismervik
Saint John the Baptist High School
West Islip, NY

Answer me when I call, O God of my right!
You gave me room when I was in distress.
Be gracious to me, and hear my prayer.
                                    (Psalm 4:1)

God,
When I need refuge,
I call you.
When I need someone to talk to,
I call you.
When I feel the world is closing around me,
I call you.
When things aren't so great,
I call you.
When I'm unhappy,
I call you.
When I'm so stressed,
I call you.
When I feel no one likes me,
I call you.

When I'm in trouble at home,
I call you.
When I need a prayer,
I call you.
When I need someone who understands me,
I call you.
When I need an immediate friend,
I call you.
When I want to get away from evil,
I call you.
When I want to see things positively,
I call you.
When I need forgiveness,
I call you.
When I need you, God,
I call you.
In thanksgiving for all your help,
I call you.

Leilani
Notre Dame High School for Girls
Chicago, IL

Dear God,
As I finish my senior year in high school, watch over me. Be with me as I go out in the real world to find myself. Give me the strength I need to stick with my education and not give up when it gets hard. I can be described as the Proverb, "Like a bird that strays from its nest is one who strays from home" (27:8). It will be hard being away, but you will always be next to me—always. When I am like the bird spreading its wings to fly, you will be the wind beneath me, holding me up. Thank you. Amen.

Michael Zurkuhlen
Saint Xavier High School
Louisville, KY

I am a firm believer that in my life, a miracle takes place each time I make it safely through a day. Being a teenager, there are many things trying to step in my way. I have to deal with relationships, schoolwork, drugs, alcohol, and all the extracurricular activities that I take part in. That is why I consider making it through a day, a miracle. To receive this miracle each day, I need to have faith. Jesus says, "Your faith has saved you" (Luke 7:50). By having faith I allow Jesus to be my salvation. I don't need anything but faith to make it through each day.

Eric M. Tepe
Elder High School
Cincinnati, OH

Out of my distress I called on the LORD;
the LORD answered me and set me in a broad place.
(Psalm 118:5)

God, we all go through some hard times.
Help us have the courage to ask for guidance.
You alone can help me most
When I feel desolate and alone.
For as sure as disasters come,
Your love shines through and lights the way.
I know you are always with me,
And I will try not to be afraid.
For it is you who will help me,
Even when I falsely accuse you of abandonment.
So I praise you now, God, because you hear me
And answer my prayers with love.

Susanna
Christian Brothers Academy
Syracuse, NY

My tongue shall tell of your righteousness
    and of your praise all day long.

(Psalm 35:28)

Forever may you reign in my life and soul,
Where you belong.
In such a divine way, you make me feel so whole,
For the sorrow and pain soon no more I shall know.
While in search for a better way, I try to avoid doing wrong.
I know that one bright day I will be strong.
As evil deceitfully stares me in the eyes
And secretly says hello,
I quickly turn away from those evil lies,
And in the wind, away it shall blow;
For I will not turn my back on you, my Lord.
That would be the biggest mistake, just plain wrong;
For you are my salvation, and thank you for the help all along.

Genesha Gutierrez
Mother Theodore Guerin High School
River Grove, IL

My God, my God, why have you forsaken me?

(Psalm 22:1)

O cross, more honest than any knight,
Prayed strong by every night,
More sacred than any rose,
So holy in thy sight alone,
Only you could hold proud,
the King of all men!

Michael Lawrence
Loyola Blakefield High School
Towson, MD

The heavens are telling the glory of God.

(Psalm 19:1)

Waves crash
they twirl swirl
upon the ripped sand
send an honor of peace
a shell lays in watch
hoping to learn
the mysteries within
yearning for nature
a systematic beauty
the earth-toned trees
reach their heavenly branches
up into the sky
pulling down the heavens of old
the untold mysteries lie within
the emerald green branches
bending, tangling, fighting
each other to become a spot
a spot of bliss
the branches house untold places to
yearn
to burn the soul
serenity making each tree see
the branch it houses
life untold places to yearn
to burn the soul
serenity making each tree see the branch
it houses a fair young pearl dove to seek
a new beginning
the dove soars from
tree to tree
through air carelessly free
uninhibited by material things
free of spins
always ongoing
dove, peace-loving friend
soars the deep blue green

unrelenting sea
watches and sees
the waves crash
they splash
upon golden brown sand
trod upon before by many
unthinking many
taken for granted
what the sand sees
the sand watches the glittering stars
above
as clouds roll in and out
the sand is there
nature is there
the constantly changing
nature
where peace, happiness, and content
dwell.

Dan Leake
University of San Diego High School
San Diego, CA

Dear God, I want to thank you for making my life comfortable and secure. I also want to thank you for blessing me with a wonderful family and many good friends. I know that I am blessed with much more than I need. But I know there are many who are not as fortunate.

So, dear God, I pray that you will help me to be friendly to those who have no friends, to reach out a helping hand to the needy, to give interest to those who get no attention, and to every now and then have a conversation with someone who has no one to talk to. May I always remember that "God is love, and those who abide in love abide in God" (1 John 4:16).

Katie Boccuti
Little Flower Catholic High School for Girls
Philadelphia, PA

God,
You gave me the sun,
That I may see,
But I cannot.
You showed your love
By setting me free,
But I am not.
The hate and fear in my life bind me,
The relationships gone bad,
And the worry of tomorrow.
I've prayed endlessly
And can feel no relief.
You told us,
"For everything there is a season,
and a time for every matter under heaven" (Ecclesiastes 3:1).
But I cannot wait.
Give me patience and inner peace.
With thanksgiving in my heart,
I praise you for the sacrifice of Christ Jesus,
"so that everyone who believes in him may not perish
but may have eternal life" (John 3:16).
Amen.

Litty Smelter
Saint Thomas More Academy
Magnolia, DE

The [servant] who had received the five talents came forward, bringing five more talents. . . . His master said to him, "Well done. . . . You have been trustworthy in a few things, I will put you in charge of many things."

(Matthew 25:20–21)

Dear God,
I know that it is not popular to put forth a lot of effort, around our friends, in most things. It's cool to lay back and do the least amount of work possible. We don't always like to develop our gifts, especially

when they don't seem useful. But God, please help us to remember that our talents are gifts from you.

Jesus, you gave a parable about talents, teaching that hiding them away will only insult and anger you. It is through investing in them, such as by practicing to be a better writer, that the talent will multiply. How will it multiply? By sharing our talents with others, we spread and double our original gifts. Jesus, you do not wish for us to bury the gifts you gave us. It would be thoughtless to never wear a shirt that a friend gave to me for my birthday. In the same way, we must wear the shirt of our talents—not showing off, but glorifying your Holy Name. This is why you gave our talents and skills to us. Amen.

Carley
Bishop McNamara High School
Forestville, MD

What if we were all the same?
Same faces, same hands, same minds.
What would our lives be?
A mirror.
A mirror of what, though?
Our fate? Our dreams? Our long-term goals?
They would *all* be the same;
the same as our family, our friends, and strangers.
How would we turn out?
Nobody knows. But
God has given us the gift of diversity!
"All things come in pairs, one opposite the other,
    and [God] has made nothing incomplete.
Each supplements the virtues of the other.
    Who could ever tire of seeing [God's] glory?" (Sirach 42:24–25)
So be who you are and be thankful for your differences.
Remember, God has given each of us our own life:
A time to live and to learn of one another.

K. S.
Bishop Manogue Catholic High School
Reno, NV

If a shepherd has a hundred sheep, and one of them has gone
astray, does he not leave the ninety-nine on the mountains
and go in search of the one that went astray?
And if he finds it, truly I tell you, he rejoices over it.
(Matthew 18:12–13)

Thank you, God, for all the world,
And everything you made,
Creatures on the land and sea,
And trees that give us shade.
Thank you for the heavens too,
The moon, the stars, and sun,
Rain and snow that bring great joy,
To each and every one.
But thank you most for us all,
The people everywhere,
For making us just like you
And showing that you care.
Even though we turn away
And evil causes sin,
Still you open up your arms,
And welcome all come in.

Alison Thomas
Our Lady of Mount Carmel High School
Baltimore, MD

The gate of heaven has opened
And many people come toward it
People with sickness, sin, and shame
All have come to ask for blessings

Now there is a mad rush
For Jesus has finally walked out
Behind him walk the apostles and saints
Then the angels sing their hymns

People cry out to him
Asking for forgiveness, healing, and comfort
I go with them too
But I walk slowly and far behind

Finally, when all is quiet and nearly all have left
I walk forward and fall on my knees at his feet
He touches my head, and my heart feels warm
Like a flame put out, but then lit once more

"Go and be happy," he tells me
I get up and start to walk away
But then I turn around and say to him
"Jesus, thank you for everything!"

He smiles a warm smile at me
Then says, "Get up and go on your way;
Your faith has made you well" (Luke 17:19)
And then adds,
"And your thanks filled me with joy!"

Nga Tran
Villa Maria Academy
Buffalo, NY

Creator of the universe,
Thank you for everything that you have given us. Thank you for our
families and friends that care so much about us. Please lead us in the
right direction in all that we do. Help us get over every burden we
come to along our path in life. Allow us to be the best persons we can
be: "For surely I know the plans I have for you, says the Lord, plans
for your welfare and not for harm, to give you a future with hope"
(Jeremiah 29:11). Thank you for this hope and a bright future. In your
name we pray. Amen.

Jarah Rider
Mercy Cross High School
Biloxi, MS

Dear God,

Thank you for all you have done for me. You created this world and loved me to the depths of the earth. I know love is important to you, for you have said: "I give you a new commandment, that you love one another. Just as I have loved you, you also should love one another" (John 13:34).

Help me, God, to try to live by this rule. It is difficult to show kindness to everyone, especially to those who are unkind to me. Let me not be ashamed to be your follower and help me to extend a kind, warm hand rather than a cold one. Help me to not get mad at the bad drivers on the road, but to control myself and try to be understanding. Help me to not argue with my mother and to show my love and gratitude for her. Instead of becoming mad at my friends, help me to resolve the problem in a loving and kind way. Aid me in following in your footsteps. Amen.

Jamie Vanessa Woodall
Academy of the Holy Names
Albany, NY

Today I thank you, God
For all the joys you bring
For rainbow in the sky
For flowers in the spring
For warmth of gentle rain
That falls from up above
For wealth of little prayers
That fill my need for love
For friends who fail me not
When I am in some need
When my despair is plain to see
Are there my soul to feed
You are so kind and gentle, God
Forgive the faults in me
And keep me ever close to you until I come to thee.

Akeisha King
West Philadelphia Catholic High School
Philadelphia, PA

What is born of the flesh is flesh, and what is born of the Spirit is spirit.
(John 3:6)

Dear God,
You gave me my hands so I would be able to reach out to others.
You gave me my voice to speak out your words
    to those who have never heard.
You gave me my ears to hear your words clearly,
    so I would be able to hear the cry of sinners,
    to wipe away their tears.
I am thankful for all that you have done for me,
    and I want to set an example for others to show them the way.
Watch over me on my path,
    so that I am able to live by the example you have given me
    and also to spread it among others.

Kia Taylor
Towson Catholic High School
Towson, MD

God of the morning dove,
    give me hope for a day full of love.
    May I do my best all through the day,
    and may I never forget to pray.
God of the morning tide,
    may I fill your heart with pride,
    for all the good deeds I will do,
    and may all the earth do good deeds, too.
God of the running deer,
    may the earth give one big cheer,
    for a new day is here.
    Let me not shed a tear.
"My help comes from the LORD,
    who made heaven and earth" (Psalm 121:2).

Ann Thomas
Catholic High School of Baltimore
Baltimore, MD

Know that the LORD is God.
>   It is he that made us, and we are his;
>   we are his people.

(Psalm 100:3)

I am here
I was created to be one
An individual am I
An individual is my creator
A creator so bold
No one can be compared to
Life, a gift that was given to the world
Life, a gift that was given to me
To me my creator is my friend
More loyal than loyal
More honorable than honorable
More powerful than powerful
Much brighter than the sun
To my creator we are the most fragile
The most precious
His light will not blind
His love will not hurt
For he is my father
For he is my savior
And I am I

Tiffany Turner
West Philadelphia Catholic High School
Philadelphia, PA

Dear God,

I understand that we do wrong and get you upset, but you don't get mad at us.

I understand that we make some mistakes and don't learn from them or sometimes lose faith in you, but you don't lose faith in us.

I understand that sometimes we don't listen to you or hear your word, but you always hear ours.

I understand that we do things to hurt you; we do hurt you, but you never hurt us.

And for this I thank you and understand that one day "the eyes of the blind shall be opened, and the ears of the deaf unstopped; then the lame shall leap like a deer, and the tongue of the speechless sing for joy" (Isaiah 35:5–6).

Even if we let you down, you are there to pick us up. And for this we give thanks to you, our God. Amen.

Shaniqua V. Lyles
Academy of Mount Saint Ursula
Bronx, NY

I have learned to be content with whatever I have. I know what it is to have little, and I know what it is to have plenty. . . . I can do all things through him who strengthens me.

(Philippians 4:11–13)

God,

Thank you for all you have given me and all you have yet to give. Thank you for opening my eyes and helping me to see that I can handle my life, and that I will handle my life. Thank you, God, for giving me the guidance to make the decisions that I have made and have yet to make. Thank you, God, for being here to listen to, watch over, and care for me. Through the wisdom of your words, I now realize that I can handle any circumstance that life deals me, and I will thank and praise you through it all.

Kymberly Lathrop
Bishop McNamara High School
Forestville, MD

The works of the Lord are wonderful.

(Sirach 11:4)

In a world of wonder that will spin, whirl, and turn,
It teaches us a lesson that we might learn.
We wonder in awe what we might do;
But what is to happen, God already knew.
All of our future rests in the palm of his hand;
We are the people of his wondrous land.
So all we have to do is take the right road;
It isn't an easy task, it is a heavy load.
But we can do it, I know we can,
Said the Son of God and the Son of Man.

Andraya Eisenman
Rosary High School
Fullerton, CA

I will give thanks to the Lord with my whole heart;
I will tell of all your wonderful deeds.

(Psalm 9:1)

Thank you, God,
for giving me parents so they can show me the way,
for providing my education because without it
    I would be narrow-minded,
for giving me my teachers and friends
    so I have shoulders to cry on in my times of need,
for putting food on the table every night,
for my clothing to keep me warm,
and last, but certainly not least, for my life,
thank you!

Michelle Emma
Academy of the Holy Names
Albany, NY

Be strong and courageous; do not be frightened or dismayed, for the LORD your God is with you wherever you go.

(Joshua 1:9)

You always stand by me, God.
When I have done wrong,
you show me forgiveness and compassion
that I may start anew.
When I am tired and angry at the world,
you give me even breath to calm my soul.
When I am weakened by pressures or doubts,
you give me strength and courage and belief in myself.
When I am frightened, lost, and alone,
you are there to listen, to guide, to ease my pain.
And so whenever I need you,
wherever I am, whatever I am doing,
I just close my eyes and open my heart,
and you give me your love.
I thank you, God.
Amen.

Liz George
Villa Maria Academy
Malvern, PA

Personal Matters

Grant me the courage,
So that I may find my path.
Help keep me safe, O God,
Away from evil's wrath.
Show me the way,
To come back to you.
I ask for forgiveness,
So I may start anew.

Each day we're being told,
Of something new to fear.
I don't know if I'm strong enough,
To question the things I hear.
I'm afraid I'm too weak,
To stand up and fight.
I'm afraid I might choose,
Wrong over right.

"Create in me a clean heart, O God,
    and put a new and right spirit within me.
Do not cast me away from your presence,
    and do not take your holy spirit from me" (Psalm 51:10–11).
I want to live,
In your love once more.
I want to have faith,
In the Spirit I adore.

Pamela S. Marsh
Catholic Central High School
Springfield, OH

O Lord, God of my salvation,
when at night, I cry out in your presence,
let my prayer come before you;
incline your ear to my cry.

(Psalm 88:1–2)

Give me the strength to fulfill my dreams;
For without you, Lord, nothing is what it seems.
Give me the wisdom to do what is right;
For without you, God, my decisions are not so bright.
Give me the courage to bring out my talents and not hide;
For without you, God, I have no pride.
Give the direction to the path of my destiny;
For without you, God, I would not know where to be.
Give me the compassion to help someone in need;
For without you, God, I would not know how to lead.
Give me motivation so I can have an honest life;
For without you, God, I would have strife.
Give me friendship for I would like to know how it feels to care;
For without you, God, I will not find my one and only.
Thank you, Lord, for all you have given me;
For with you, God, is where I want to be.

Jenny Torres
Notre Dame High School for Girls
Chicago, IL

Every day things occur in this world that shake my faith and test my beliefs. I see things happening like famine and civil wars, and things that hit close to home like cancer and AIDS. I find myself constantly questioning life. I wonder, God, why you let these things occur? God, please help me to stand firm in my beliefs and in my faith through times of question and doubt. You said, "Remember, I am with you always, to the end of the age" (Matthew 28:20). Help me to keep remembering that somewhere in your great plan, it all works out. Amen.

Mark S. Wooding and Jeff Miazga
Xavier High School
Middletown, CT

Who can own all the rocks?
Who can own the trees?
Who can steal a honeycomb
From some angry bees?

Who can divide the ocean up?
Who can split the earth?
Who can read all the books
And tell me what they're worth?

God grant me the serenity
To understand these things.
God grant me the patience
To hear the angel sing.

God grant me the lovingness
To hear the homeless and the poor.
God grant me the willingness
To open every door.

God grant me the intelligence
To explore all of my dreams.
God grant me the courage
To see what love really means.

God grant me the privilege
To come and see you one day.
God grant me the inspiration
To get on my knees and pray.

"God so loved the world
that he gave his only Son,
so that everyone who believes in him may not perish
but may have eternal life" (John 3:16).

Constance Barbara David
Catholic High School of Baltimore
Baltimore, MD

Save me, God, from my troubles and protect me from my fears.
Listen to my prayers for mercy and dry my many tears.
For without you I am alone, without you I cannot live.
But with you my life thrives and there is so much I can give.
When I feel energized and joyful, I know you're still behind me,
When I feel a bit confused, I know you're right beside me.
When I'm lost and lonely, you take my hand and lead me.
I'm hungry for your love and I know that you will feed me.

Angela Fisher
Catholic Central High School
Springfield, OH

The human mind plans the way,
but the LORD directs the steps.

(Proverbs 16:9)

Dear Holy Spirit,
Be with me today, so that I may prepare myself for tomorrow.
Guide me away from all temptation,
especially that which comes from my peers.
Help me to glorify God today and always,
in all that I do.
Help me to work hard, and to never be lazy.
Allow me to follow my heart, and not the crowd.
Turn me away from such evil things
as violence, irresponsible sex, drugs, and alcohol.
Turn me toward love, friends, family, faith, and God.
Amen.

Gregory Ross Sanders
John Carroll Catholic High School
Birmingham, AL

God,
It's not even the middle of the school year, and already I count the days until summer. I'm just worn out and tired: tired of school, tired of parents, and sometimes tired of my friends. It seems everyone expects too much out of me. I'm just out of energy. The only thing I have to look forward to is the weekends. I know if I reach out to you, you can help me get through this year. God "restores my soul. [God] leads me in right paths" (Psalm 23:3). Amen.

Lara Obert
John Carroll Catholic High School
Birmingham, AL

And now, O Lord, what do I wait for?
　My hope is in you.

(Psalm 39:7)

God, my life seems to become more confusing by the day.
I get upset over stupid little things
and take it out on the people I care about.
I'm sick of talking about colleges and majors
and what I want to do with my life,
because I'm not done being a kid.
But I want to be treated like an adult.
Amidst my thoughts and worries and actions,
I feel like I'm losing touch with what's really important.
God, please help me to remember the good in my life,
my family, my friends, myself.
Because when I do, I get this weird feeling
that everything will probably work out.

E. E. M.
Bishop McNamara High School
Forestville, MD

Hear my prayer, O LORD;
   let my cry come to you.
Do not hide your face from me
      in the day of my distress.
Incline your ear to me;
      answer me speedily.

(Psalm 102:1–2)

God,
Here I stand full of fear,
for at this moment ends my senior year.
Tomorrow holds my college venture,
when I leave early September.
A new freedom is what the future holds,
and all the pressures—I have been told.
I pray for guidance and divine light,
for life on my own will be a fight.
Food to fix and laundry to do,
life will be hard for a few.
Papers to write, books to read,
"time management" is what I really need.
The prayer that I pray is for your ear,
it comes from the heart and is truly sincere.
I pray for patience, I pray for knowledge,
that's something I'll need to get through college.
I pray that you hear my humble prayer,
and answer me speedily, "I'll always be there."

Keenon James
Bishop McNamara High School
Forestville, MD

What I think counts is
if you are you and you stay that way.
When you are you,
you are unique and different.

What I think counts is
when you don't judge others.
When you judge others and you don't like to be judged,
why do you do it?

What I think counts is
when you do your best.
When you do your best,
you succeed.

"To whom then will you compare me,
or who is my equal? says the Holy One" (Isaiah 40:25).

Tara McDonnell
Our Lady of Perpetual Help
Ellicott City, MD

Hi, God!
There is so much going on in my life right now,
I feel like I need to speed up, or be left behind.
It seems like everyone is rushing around,
but I don't know what the big hurry is.
Please help me to not get caught up in the rigors of daily life,
but to remember what you said in your word,
"For everything there is a season,
and a time for every matter under heaven" (Ecclesiastes 3:1).
Thank you for helping me to slow down
and remember what is important.

Emily Schrag
Holy Trinity Student Chapel
Ypsilanti, MI

Protect me, O God, for in you I take refuge.
I say to the LORD, "You are my Lord;
  I have no good apart from you.

(Psalm 16:1–2)

Dear God,
Today I will need your help. I know I must make some very difficult decisions. So in you I take refuge. Please help me to make the correct decisions for things that we as teenagers face, such as peer pressure and friendships. I say to you, God, you are my only good. I love you, and again, please help me.

Erin M. Keelin

Our Lady Star of the Sea Church

Port Isabel, TX

God,
At times I feel lost, alone, and confused.
I'm not sure which path life will lead me down,
or how I'll ever know which one to choose.
So, God, help me to remember:
  "Our steps are made firm by the LORD,
    when he delights in our way;
  though we stumble, we shall not fall headlong,
    for the LORD holds us by the hand" (Psalm 37:23–24).
I know you are beside me, God,
but at times I become discouraged and forget.
Help me to put my full trust in you,
for I know the path that I will follow
was paved long before I even knew your name.

Kristen Jungen

Aquinas High School

La Crosse, WI

Come to me, all you that are weary and are carrying heavy burdens, and I will give you rest.

(Matthew 11:28)

God.
Help me to find you when I am overwhelmed.
I seek you for relief.
Let me seek your comfort when I am drained, energy-less, and tired.
Teach me the patience and endurance that I need
    when I am ready to quit.
Push me when I try to turn away from what I must do
    for what I want to do.
Show me what I should learn now to help me later on.
Focus my eyes on the future.
Tell me what I must do to always be in your presence
    during tiresome and stressful times.
I ask this in Jesus' name. Amen.

Brian Daniel Burris
Jesuit High School
Carmichael, CA

All who exalt themselves will be humbled, but all who humble themselves will be exalted.

(Luke 18:14)

Sometimes it is difficult to be a mature and responsible Christian. I know that everyone is not perfect, but it is our responsibility to do the best we can. The fact that I am not perfect makes me work harder in all that I do to achieve the highest goals I set. We need your help to guide us and support us.

God, help us to be humble. Encourage us to accept ourselves for who we are. Let us realize we are human and can make mistakes; we all do. Our mistakes are lessons for the future. They help us to make better decisions and teach us that we are not better than anyone else.

We should never put others down for their mistakes. We can learn from them as well as from our own.

Motivate us to be proud of our accomplishments in a healthy way. Help us stop before making people feel inferior to us by boasting about our luxuries. Allow us to appreciate what we and others have and what we and others can do.

Dawn Harrison
Stella Maris High School
Rockaway Park, NY

If any of you is lacking in wisdom, ask God, who gives to all generously and ungrudgingly, and it will be given you.
(James 1:5)

God,
I come to you at this time asking for your guidance and your wisdom. I am confused as to what I should do regarding my college choices. There are so many new decisions, so many new issues to face. And I am not able to think clearly on what the best choices are.

Please guide me and give me the wisdom to sort through all the many things I have to face. I am asking that you open my ears and tune my spirit that I may hear and understand the advisors you send my way. Help me, God, to listen deeply to my parents, teachers, college advisors, and friends so that I can get enough information to make good choices. God, please give me the wisdom to make choices that are right and not just easy.

As always I thank you for your love and mercy that has supported me in the past, and I thank you for your grace and your love that will endure to the end of all time. Amen.

Ngonzi Crushshon
Longwood Academy
Chicago, IL

God,
You watched her, with those *things* in her hands on the verge of . . .
You saw her delicately trace her veins with a blade, daring to press
harder. You heard her distressed plea directed toward no one and
everyone at once: "I cannot take it anymore!" You winced as she
tensely pushed harder into the skin, but suddenly, a noise. She stopped.
Her cat? Her parents? No, the noise was your voice: "Do not worry
about anything, but in everything by prayer and supplication with
thanksgiving let your requests be made known to God" (Philippians
4:6). She thought she was going crazy: God talking? And to her of all
people? Yet, she could not shrug it off; instead, she obeyed. She put
down the scissors and talked to you.

How many teenagers have thought it, resorted to it, attempted it—
suicide? I do not wish to know, but God, I am overjoyed to know that
you, you are there, even in our most dire times. God, give teenagers
the strength to turn to you when they think suicide is the only option,
and give them the humbleness to not only hear your voice but obey it,
when you call to help. Amen.

Jeanne
Gabriel Richard High School
Riverview, MI

If I have all faith, so as to remove mountains, but do not have love, I am
nothing. If I give away all my possessions, . . . but do not have love, I
gain nothing.
(1 Corinthians 13:2–3)

Dear God,
Just as I say a little prayer each day, this one also comes from my heart.
Today I'm praying that everyone has an open heart to love somebody,
because without love we are nothing. Dear God, I'm also asking that
you help me to keep an open heart. Please help me to have never-
ending unconditional love for those whom I already love, and help me
to open my heart to others who are striving for love. Dear Lord, please
help me to know that I need to love to live a good, full, complete life.

Amy A. Andraska
Saint Joseph Parish
Black River Falls, WI

I have said these things to you so that my joy may be in you, and that your joy may be complete.

(John 15:11)

God,
Every day I become aware of the problems of the world. Why? Why do bad things happen to good people? It is difficult to understand your mysteries.

God, you know that most of the time, human eyes do not see essential things. You tell us, "I have said these things to you so that my joy may be in you, and that your joy may be complete." God, help me be able to find you everywhere. Explain everything to me so that I may enlighten my understanding. Show me the way, and if it has obstacles, help me understand that they do have a reason.

Guide me, because then, every time I fall, I will have the security that you are there with me. Carry me in your arms through this journey, because by being held by you, your joy—a complete one—will reign in my soul. Give me the strength and joy to walk with you, because then I will be a better human being and an example of all your preaching. Thus you will help me achieve sanctification. Amen.

Natalia Canto
Academia María Reina
San Juan, PR

God, give me the strength and power needed to vanquish my foes in the awesome game of football; increase my ability to run fast and block well. Help me to make my reads on defense and play my pass coverages well.

Let the opposing team get no positive yards or points. Make our running game furious and strong and our passing game accurate. Help my teammates and me to tackle with form, so that the other team's running backs cough up the ball, and we return it for six.

"Let God rise up, let his enemies be scattered" (Psalm 68:1).

Mike Caputo
Coyle and Cassidy High School
Taunton, MA

God who loves us,
You give me courage and strength
When hardships come my way.
Help me to put my faith in you always.
You comfort and encourage me when all seems lost.
In times of loneliness, I know you are near.
Help me to understand others as you do me.
You give me peace of heart,
And love me despite my faults and sins.
Help me to listen to my conscience.
You grant me the joys and beauty of nature,
Your eternal love is shown here.
Help me to appreciate all that you've created.
You safely guard me in your embrace,
I place myself in your gracious care.
Help me to keep watch over others.
You are my hope and inspiration,
My guiding hand and savior.
Help me to live out your message of love.
"Blessed be the LORD,
    for he has wondrously shown his steadfast love to me
    when I was beset as a city under siege.
I had said in my alarm,
    'I am driven far from your sight.'
But you heard my supplications
    when I cried out to you for help" (Psalm 31:21–22).

Christina Tracey Czap
Mercy High School
Middletown, CT

God who loves us, when we really love someone, we love them for who they are, not for what they're not or what we want them to be. Help us to love like this: "Love is kind; love is not envious or boastful or arrogant or rude. It does not insist on its own way . . . but rejoices in the truth" (1 Corinthians 13:4–6).

Tim Johnson
Saint Joseph Parish
Black River Falls, WI

Dear Christ,
Please help all teens all over the world understand that you love us.
Even when depression sets in and we can't understand why you would
let that happen, help us understand that you are here with us and
inside us to support and guide us. You said, "I am with you always, to
the end of the age" (Matthew 28:20). Please, Christ, reach down with
your hands and guide teens in need that have no one to guide them
through these hard times, especially with depression. Help them to
understand that they are loved unconditionally. Amen.

Patrick
Coyle and Cassidy High School
Taunton, MA

Lord God,
Help to guide me in the right directions.
Help me realize which choices are wise.
Help me live out your Gospel.
Guide me to where I am needed.
Guide me on the right path.
Guide me from evil.
Encourage me to spread your word.
Encourage me to come to you when I need help.
Encourage me to have faith in you.

Father, people have believed that you were a "do nothing" God.
Help me to trust in your name.
I believe that you will always love me,
but please help me remember this in the future.

"For I will leave in the midst of you a people humble and lowly.
They shall seek refuge in the name of the LORD—
the remnant of Israel;
they shall do no wrong and utter no lies" (Zephaniah 3:12–13).
Amen.

Amanda Renée Smith
Catholic High School of Baltimore
Baltimore, MD

There should be for one of them an angel, a mediator.

(Job 33:23)

God, I am afraid that one day I'll give the wrong advice
and something very bad will happen as a result.
How am I supposed to convince someone
who is contemplating suicide that they are truly loved?
When someone who just found out that they are pregnant
comes to me, what do I do?
When my friends are suffering from eating disorders
and serious illnesses, how do I comfort them?
God, grant me the wisdom to say and do the right things.

Kathryn Lessard
Saint Thomas More Academy
Magnolia, DE

Save me, O God, . . .
I have come into deep waters,
and the flood sweeps over me.

(Psalm 69:1–2)

God, so many pressures seem too difficult to deal with.
From parents to school to just growing up,
I cannot deal with these things alone.
Please save me from drowning in this sea of stresses.
Help me to bear my cross,
and calm the tumultuous waters of my heart and mind
so that I might be able to serve you and others better.

Mary Frances Mayo
Bishop McNamara High School
Forestville, MD

As tip-off approaches, send your Holy Spirit down upon us. "Blessed be the LORD, my rock, who trains my hands for war, and my fingers for battle" (Psalm 144:1). Allow us to use the talents you have given us to the best of our ability. Help our feet to be swift and our minds to be focused. Guide our passes to the receivers and our shots to the basket. Ease our nerves and keep us free from injury. No matter what the outcome, may sportsmanship prevail so that at the end of the game, we can give glory to your name. Amen.

Jenna Hayes
Roncalli High School
Indianapolis, IN

Do not judge, and you will not be judged.

(Luke 6:37)

Somehow, God, that's not how things seem to work at my high school. I try not to ever judge people by what they're wearing, how they act, talk, or look either. But I feel as though others are passing judgment, analyzing, and scrutinizing me! Each new day brings another chance for me to simply be myself, who I really am. This does not mean that the pressures I feel are any different from anyone else's.

It sure was easier being younger. Playing Capture the Flag and Kick the Can with my neighborhood friends was certainly much more fun! Those were the days of childhood when everyone was friends and there were no cliques. We formed groups and hung around with one another, having common interests along with sharing kindness toward one another.

I guess what I'm seeking here, God, is strength to guide me through these rough teenage times that really are seemingly unnecessary evils. Please help me focus on the important issues: truly being the best example for others that I'm capable of. Just consider me an instrument in your "Tool Belt of Teen Teachers." Thanks!

Sincerely in Scripture,

M. E. G.
Saint Patrick Church
Troy, OH

God,
Give me courage.
Jesus said, "Take courage;
I have conquered the world" (John 16:33).
But having courage is hard.
I need courage to say what I want.
I need to know that what I say
can and may make a difference even though I'm young.
I need courage to act as I should.
I need to know that I must do the right thing
no matter how hard it may be.
I need courage to face my problems head-on.
I need to learn not to keep it all inside.
Help me, God. This courage thing is tough.

Carrie Smietanka
Lake Michigan Catholic High School
Saint Joseph, MI

God,
Please help all those who are going through hardships at home,
especially those whose parents are going through divorce.
Help them survive the arguments and depression.
Help them to look at the world and know
that tomorrow will be better.
Even if they go through the deepest darkness,
they will not be afraid,
God, for you are with them.
"He leads me beside still waters;
    he restores my soul.
He leads me in right paths. . . .
Even though I walk through the darkest valley,
    I fear no evil;
for you are with me" (Psalm 23:2–4).

Jennifer Caban
Saint John the Baptist High School
West Islip, NY

For thinking that in their secret sins they were unobserved
behind a dark curtain of forgetfulness,
they were scattered, terribly alarmed,
and appalled by specters.

(Wisdom of Solomon 17:3)

Dear all-knowing God,
Help me to notice my hidden sins when I dismiss them.
Make obvious the things I do wrong when I ignore what I've done.
Help me notice when I say words I shouldn't.
When I lie to myself about things I know I have done wrong,
let me see the truth.
Help me to be kind to those that I don't like.
Help me to respect those that I am rude to.
Help me to love everyone as I love myself.
Bring out my sins when I try to hide them away.
Do all this so I may repent and make right what I've done wrong.

Brie Whitmire
Saint Gertrude High School
Richmond, VA

Those who wait for the LORD shall renew their strength,
they shall mount up with wings like eagles.

(Isaiah 40:31)

In life sometimes things get harder, and we start to get frustrated. This happens for everybody. We get so overwhelmed that we want to just give up. If we trust in God for help, our strength shall be renewed. We should never let anything get the best of us. And when things feel impossible and the world is caving in on us, we can just keep our head up, work through it, and expect God's assistance. Just like Samson with his hair or Moses and his walking stick—both needed God's help, and when they knew they'd get it, extraordinary things happened for them. Nobody goes their whole life without any problems. God knows this and cares. So we can just believe and we will succeed.

Jon Eddinger
Towson Catholic High School
Towson, MD

God, I often find it easy to find the faults in others. I hope that you can help me deal with my own personal flaws before noticing those of others. I am reminded of the Bible story of a woman who was caught in adultery. They were going to stone her when Jesus said, "Let anyone among you who is without sin be the first to throw a stone at her" (John 8:7). Everyone left her alone because they all had sinned. Help me to not "throw a stone," and to just concentrate on making myself a better person.

Jim Crowley
Coyle and Cassidy High School
Taunton, MA

Blessed is anyone who will eat bread in the kingdom of God!
(Luke 14:15)

Dear God, please bless all of us drivers as we seek to reach your kingdom. Please point out to us the freeway that leads to eternal life. Please do not let us miss any of the road signs. Please help us to get off at the correct off-ramp, so that we will arrive in time to dine at your table in the kingdom of heaven. We ask this in Jesus' name. Amen.

Jake Deterding
Jesuit High School
Carmichael, CA

Dear God,
I am aware that I appear as a quiet person to those who do not know me. This is a valid observation; I often do keep to myself. Yet I am not always serious. I love to joke, laugh, and make others laugh. I possess the ability to make others laugh, but I only feel comfortable sharing my gift with those closest to me. Please help me to do as Peter instructed, "Like good stewards of the manifold grace of God, serve one another with whatever gift each of you has received" (1 Peter 4:10). Amen.

Susan Giza
Divine Child High School
Dearborn, MI

Thank you, Lord, for all the gifts you give me, even "You have pain now; but I will see you again, and your hearts will rejoice, and no one will take your joy from you" (John 16:22).

Thank you, God, for all the gifts you give me, even the gift of sadness. Help me understand that being sad is a normal process of life and that if I don't understand it right now, eventually everything will clear out and it will help me overcome other situations that will come up later in my life. Give me the strength to cope with every challenge that appears in my way and to accept it with open arms. I know that afterward you will bring me the joy, dear Jesus, that I need to keep on going. Amen.

Claudia Calderón-Pacheco
Academia María Reina
San Juan, PR

God, I know that this passage is true because of firsthand experience: "A wise child makes a glad father, but a foolish child is a mother's grief" (Proverbs 10:1). Being foolish was one experience that I would never like to encounter again in my life. So, God, I beg you to never let me even come close to being a foolish son again. And, God, if you don't want to answer my prayer, at least do it for my health, because my mom will kill me next time it happens. Amen.

Adam Binsfeld
Aquinas High School
La Crosse, WI

Dear God,
Help me express the gifts you have given me and not hide them in shame. Let me help others by using my gifts. "No one after lighting a lamp puts it in a cellar, . . . your whole body is full of light" (Luke 11:33–34). May my light shine. Amen.

Shannon Shaw
Immaculata Academy
Hamburg, NY

The people stood by, watching [Jesus on the cross]; but the leaders scoffed at him, saying, "He saved others; let him save himself if he is the Messiah of God, his chosen one.

(Luke 23:35)

A lot of times I get yelled at, even for things I had nothing to do with. A lot of times not even my parents will believe me and stand by me. And I think, "How humiliating."

Sometimes I get punished or smacked in front of my friends or that really fine guy I've been trying to go out with. And I think, "How humiliating."

A lot of times I don't pay attention in class or when someone is talking, and I get asked to answer a question I don't know and end up looking like an idiot. I think, "How humiliating."

Sometimes I do, say, or wear something that is wrong and inappropriate at church, and I get caught by the pastor or some other high leader. They might call me rebellious or maybe even demon possessed. I may think, "How humiliating."

All these things, whether they might happen every day or maybe just once in a great while, I think of as the most humiliating and awful things that can ever happen to a person. They don't even come close to all the humiliation, pain, and suffering that Jesus went through when he carried the cross in front of the whole city and then hung on it to die just for our sins. They mocked him, spit at him, and even his own disciple denied him. But Jesus didn't run away. He stood bold and courageous and took all that humiliation and pain for the love of us.

So I just pray, God, that you may strengthen me and help me remember all you had your only son do for us. I pray that you may help me to be more like him and understand why I go through all this. In your precious name, I pray. Amen.

Adriana Rodriguez
Notre Dame High School for Girls
Chicago, IL

I am coming to you, God, with a clear heart and soul. I know you may not answer my prayer, but I know you will hear it.

My prayer is a prayer of asking for forgiveness. The Bible states: "Six days you shall labor and do all your work. But the seventh day is a Sabbath to the LORD your God; you shall not do any work" (Deuteronomy 5:13–14).

Most of the time on the Sabbath, I don't show any respect to you, God. I fill my Sundays up with work and play, without any thoughts for my God.

I ask for your full-hearted forgiveness for my neglect of the Sabbath day. I will try hard to give some special moments on the Sabbath from now on.

Nicholas Hill
Bishop Manogue Catholic High School
Reno, NV

In everything do to others as you would have them do to you.
(Matthew 7:12)

Dear God let me find patience among my friends.
Dear God let me practice patience with my teachers.
Dear God let me learn patience from my elders.
Dear God let me have patience with my family.
Dear God let me be patient with myself.

Let me treat others with strength and courage. Especially those who are less fortunate than I am. Inspire me to seek out those in need.

Please help me forgive those who haven't been patient with me, and forgive me for my impatience with others. I ask this through Christ. Amen.

Niclas Murk
Jesuit High School
Carmichael, CA

I have prayed for you that your own faith may not fail.
(Luke 22:32)

God,
Help us to keep our faith in you,
Not to betray you,
To keep our promises,
Not to lie,
Follow you always,
And not let our fears get in the way
of our judgment of what is right.
Amen.

Michelle Kreafle
Catholic High School of Baltimore
Baltimore, MD

Love is patient; love is kind.
(1 Corinthians 13:4)

God, please help me to acknowledge the love in my life, not only the love that I feel for others but also the love that others feel for me.

Help me to not make the mistake of many teenagers who search for love in the wrong places and in actions such as premarital sex. Help me to be honest with myself about the love I feel, and not to hide it or tell myself that something is love when it isn't. Allow me to see the difference between true love and all the other feelings that I am feeling. As we are bombarded by society's views on love, help me and all the other people in the world understand the value of true love. Help me to act in the way that you desire. Amen.

Katie Nelson
Saint Gertrude High School
Richmond, VA

At the set time that I appoint
  I will judge with equity.
When the earth totters, with all its inhabitants,
    it is I who keep its pillars steady.
                                    (Psalm 75:2–3)

Every year over 5,000 people between the ages of 14 and 24 commit suicide, and over 500,000 more try to. I'm one of the people that has tried. Please give me the wisdom to realize that you, God, will judge us and that we are worth living. Give us the strength to survive, to make it through this hard time when we feel unloved and lonely. I look for a way to ease the pain. Every time that I have hurt myself, it was my way of asking for your help and advice. Help me to live. Thank you, God. I love you. Amen.

Shawn Morales
Coyle and Cassidy High School
Taunton, MA

About three o'clock Jesus cried with a loud voice, . . . "My God, my God, why have you forsaken me?"
                                    (Matthew 27:46)

Jesus, sometimes I think I know just how you were feeling that day. I, too, have moments when I feel God has forgotten about me, such as when my grandmother died despite all my prayers. In my heart I know God is always with me, and I am truly sorry for those times when I asked God for favors that were really quite selfish. Just give me a little more faith.

Christopher Miley
Northeast Catholic High School
Philadelphia, PA

Our God forever and ever.
He will be our guide forever.

(Psalm 48:14)

My Creator, help me when I feel unloved, to find love.
When I feel left out from the world, help me feel wanted.
When I am sad, help me be with those that let me see happiness.
When I feel scared, help me feel stronger than the fear.
When I feel lonely, help me feel comforted.
When I feel depressed, help me realize
    that there is more to life than this feeling.
God, I know you are there to give me strength
    and to guide me through these feelings.
Amen.

Stephanie Ann LaBella
John Carroll High School
Fort Pierce, FL

God,
Thank you for making me unique. Only you could create a world full of such different people. "When I look at your heavens, the work of your fingers, the moon and the stars that you have established; what are human beings that you are mindful of them, mortals that you care for them?" (Psalm 8:3–4). I ask for your assistance; help me to stay my own person forever. God, help me to remain an individual like no one else. Sometimes I am tempted to listen to others and ignore your callings, even though you know what is best for me. Sometimes I pay too much attention to the likes, dislikes, desires, and plans of others and neglect to acknowledge and recognize my own. God, remind me that I must be myself to truly love the real me. Amen.

Beth Salonia
Mercy High School
Middletown, CT

Friends and Family

Faithful friends are a sturdy shelter:
   whoever finds one has found a treasure.
Faithful friends are beyond price;
   no amount can balance their worth.

(Sirach 6:14–15)

God, help me to be a true friend to those I love. Help me to be a brother to all my friends and to be strong when they are hurt. Help me to always remain loyal to my true friends and to never bring harm upon them, for I would no more wish to harm them than I would my own kin. I pray to you to help them as you help me, and to allow our love for each other to grow more into a state of solidarity each day. Amen.

Joseph Sullivan
Peoria Notre Dame High School
Peoria, IL

Thank you, Creator of the universe. "We give thanks to you, O God; we give thanks" (Psalm 75:1). I say this because though sometimes I don't appreciate them, you gave me parents who keep me from being like friends of mine whom I pray to you about: those who are pregnant, alone, uneducated, and most hurtful—unloved. I love you because you know me better than anyone else. I share with you my dreams and my faults. I will always ask for tomorrow to be as lovely as the day before. Thank you for being my best friend in a world where one is hard to find.

L. K.
West Philadelphia Catholic High School
Philadelphia, PA

Dear God,
I write this prayer, not for me,
because things are okay at home.
But I send it to you for many others
who are caught in the middle.

I need someone to talk to,
someone who will understand,
someone who will listen,
and someone who will care.
I have a really big problem,
and I fear I might be the cause.
My parents have been fighting,
so much I cannot sleep.
Try to help me know
just what is going on.
Is this my fault?
Am I the cause?
I need to know right now.
Please help me understand,
while you are listening and caring.
"To you, O LORD, I lift up my soul.
O my God, in you I trust" (Psalm 25:1–2).
Love,
Jamie

Jamie Lynn Press
Saint John the Baptist High School
West Islip, NY

I am continually with you;
    you hold my right hand.
You guide me with your counsel,
    and afterward you will receive me with honor.
                    (Psalm 73:23–24)

God, I need some advice.
Although grade school was fun,
People told me high school was twice as nice.

But God, I'm not so sure that's true,
And right now I don't know what to do.
I was told that in high school I would make new memories,
But now I'm thinking that was all a tease.
Now I feel alone,
Like I'm going through everything on my own.
I really need a friend,
But some old friendships are too broken to mend.
So I'm asking you, God,
Please help me to see
That no matter what,
You will always be with me.

Jaclyn Chentfant
Mount Mercy Academy
Buffalo, NY

Today I found out again that friends aren't always perfect.
I told a friend something in confidence,
Only to hear it repeated by someone I hardly know.
I can talk to you, God.
You are my perfect friend.
I can ask you anything.
How should I treat my friend?
Should I forgive her?
"If anyone strikes you on the right cheek,
turn the other also" (Matthew 5:39).
How many times should I forgive her?
You told Peter,
"Not seven times, but . . . seventy-seven times" (Matthew 18:22).
God, give me the strength to forgive and forgive again,
the patience to be a caring friend,
and help me to be more like my perfect friend.

Susan Rae Janiszewski
Lake Michigan Catholic High School
Saint Joseph, MI

Mom and Dad:
You've been married longer than I've been here. You married because you were in love with each other, and you knew that God put you both on this earth to be together. So before you make this drastic decision about separating, remember this: "Love is patient; love is kind; love is not envious or boastful or arrogant or rude; . . . it does not rejoice in wrongdoing, but rejoices in the truth. It bears all things, believes all things, hopes all things, endures all things" (1 Corinthians 13:4–7). These words mean a lot because love brought you together and will keep you together.

So, God, after hearing these words, please remember you brought them together with love and that will last forever. So aid them while they are going through troubles. And always be with them. Amen.

Matt
Peoria Notre Dame High School
Peoria, IL

Faithful friends are a sturdy shelter:
    whoever finds one has found a treasure.
Faithful friends are beyond price;
    no amount can balance their worth.
                    (Sirach 6:14–15)

Dear God,
As this new day begins, please help us to stay focused and understanding throughout the day. Help us to get to know someone we may not normally accept or understand. Help us find a friend in someone we may not normally see and to treat them with the same respect we ask others to give us. Amen.

Kim Miazga
Mercy High School
Middletown, CT

Dear God,
I have this feeling inside of me, a feeling so perfect and joyous. It's the best gift I've ever given and the best I've ever received—the gift of love. Through many times, both good and bad, we've been together and have shared precious moments that I know in my heart will last forever. I know how teens can be, but trust me, God, the two of us are special. It goes way beyond the physical attraction. I love him for who he is, all that he stands for, all he has accomplished, his humbleness, compassion, and understanding. But not just this. No, you can never fully love a person without loving the whole person.

I love him for his faults too, because that's what makes him who he is. For what we both lack, we make up for in each other. I see the truth in his eyes that nobody else can see, and the smile on our faces, the simple touch of our hands. They all may be little, but the little things mean the most. We are truly lifelong companions, best friends, and soul mates. Love "bears all things, believes all things, hopes all things, endures all things. . . . Faith, hope, and love abide, these three; and the greatest of these is love" (1 Corinthians 13:7,13). These words express my feelings exactly. I love him so much, and I know he loves me. So please, God, grant us the blessing that we will always and forever be. Amen.

Jackie Schrader
Rosary High School
Fullerton, CA

Those who trouble their households will inherit wind,
    and the fool will be servant to the wise.
                                    (Proverbs 11:29)

God, help me to live kindly. Many times I forget that the faces I see around me are real people. I forget that they have feelings too. Help me so that I do not turn my friends against me by saying something before I think. Help me to live as you would live if you were on Earth. Let me hold on to my friends and keep them for my whole life. Amen.

T. K. K.
Christian Brothers Academy
Syracuse, NY

My companion . . .
   violated a covenant with me!

(Psalm 55:20)

Oh God,
please hear my prayers.
I am so confused and
I carry angry grudges.
I need strength, for my best friend has betrayed me.
We both went to church and praised you, God.
She knew my deepest secrets,
and she was the one I confided in.
And after years of this, I turn my back
and my friend tells lies about me.
Please, God, just send us relief.
Make my friend see the wrong she's done.
But have pity on her, for she doesn't know
how deeply she's wounded me.
I trust you, my God. Amen.

Jessica Crystal Roman
Saint Raymond Academy
Bronx, NY

The Big Picture

Dear God,
Give us the strength to live each day with the goodness you seek,
and help us to remember that this is not the life we are made for.
Let us remember that it is here we decide
if we shall live life eternal with you, and
that prosperity in this life means nothing in the next.
Help those who are in need.
Let them remember that the suffering they endure for you
will not go unnoticed,
and that those who boast of success, but lead empty lives,
will suffer.
Let us live our lives with humble love,
and take strife and misery modestly.
Let us rejoice with our families,
for even if we seemingly have nothing—
no clothes, no money, no shelter, no food—
we undoubtedly have an incredible love.
And if we seem to have everything, but lack love,
we have nothing.
Grant that we remember your words:
"Better is a dinner of vegetables where love is
than a fatted ox and hatred with it" (Proverbs 15:17).
We ask you this in the name of the Father, and of the Son,
and of the Holy Spirit. Amen.

Andrew Catauro
Bishop Hendricken High School
Warwick, RI

I say to you, Love your enemies and pray for those who persecute you, so that you may be children of your Father in heaven; for he makes his sun rise on the evil and on the good, and sends rain on the righteous and on the unrighteous.

(Matthew 5:44–45)

The pressures of another day take a toll
On a tired mind in a tired world.
Heads hang heavy,
Fists clench,
Thoughts pound.
When the boot kicks your teeth in
And it all seems like a waste,
You turn the page
And feel the words
Trembling in your soul.
"Let it go," he tells you.
"Forgive, and remember that I am here.
The sun will rise another day
On you *and* all your enemies."
Lift your head,
And find a promise of peace
In the heart of the Savior,
Who died on a cross for the sins
Of you
And your enemies.

David Grillo
Muskegon Catholic Central High School
Muskegon, MI

Dear God,
you said,
"Do not worry about tomorrow,
for tomorrow will bring worries of its own" (Matthew 6:34).
But many times
I find it hard to be peaceful.
I am occupied with
school, friends, college,
even praying to you.
Please help me
to understand and
to follow your words,
to allow myself time
to be filled with only you,
and to believe
that you will take care of me.
Help me to realize that
I do not have to take on the world
by myself.
Amen.

J. L. H.
Bishop McNamara High School
Forestville, MD

Dear God,
Please provide me with the wisdom to make the decisions needed to fulfill my duty as a peacemaker on Earth. Help me to be kind in all my actions as well as my words. "Blessed are those who are persecuted for righteousness' sake, for theirs is the kingdom of heaven" (Matthew 5:10). Let me embrace those who are shoved to the side, and because of them, let me be thankful for what I possess. Please, God, enable me to instill more benevolence in the world so that we may live as wonderful children of God. Amen.

Corey M. Price
Brother Martin High School
New Orleans, LA

Do not rejoice when your enemies fall,
and do not let your heart be glad when they stumble.
(Proverbs 24:17)

God, sometimes it is easy to get caught up in how people look, what they say or do, who they hang out with, or how much money they have. It is easy to see when others fail, especially when we are looking for it. During this time in our lives, it is easy to make ourselves feel better by putting others down.

God, help us to choose the difficult road instead of the easy one. Help us to not judge others for who they aren't or rejoice in their failings. Help us to see the good in everyone, for we all make mistakes and are constantly trying to overcome our pasts. None of us is perfect.

Someday in heaven we will all have perfect wings, and our failings, mistakes, and differences will not matter. To get our wings, we must first learn to rejoice in the good of life. We must learn to love and help others, to think of someone else before ourselves. We must trust in you, God. Help us open our minds and hearts to those we find difficult to love. Help us to be strong enough to deal with our own failings without trying to point out others' to boost ourselves up. You know our true hearts, God. This day is yours.

Ingrid Torres
Roncalli High School
Indianapolis, IN

Dear God,
There are many problems in the world today, but if I have the courage to face these problems, please give me the strength. If I have the strength, please give me the courage. If I have both the strength and the courage, give me your blessing. And if I have neither, please give me a guardian angel. For what Jesus said, "The spirit indeed is willing, but the flesh is weak" (Matthew 26:41), is always true no matter who you are, because we all need God.

Eric J. Pitre
Brother Martin High School
New Orleans, LA

Dear God,

Help us with the gift of tolerance. Help us to accept and respect our brothers' and sisters' differences. Help us to follow the light of your path to the virtue of unconditional love that you so graciously spread upon each of us. With deep faith we ask for the strength to do away with injustice and the prejudices that have already been instilled in us. May we turn away from negative media images and focus more on your teachings. God, please guide us to be more like the father of the prodigal son, a father who "saw him and was filled with compassion; he ran and put his arms around him and kissed him" (Luke 15:20), even though his son had betrayed him. God, you are our guiding light. Amen.

Khadija Goding
Stella Maris High School
Rockaway Park, NY

Therefore you have no excuse, whoever you are, when you judge others; for in passing judgment on another you condemn yourself, because you, the judge, are doing the very same things.
(Romans 2:1)

God, help us to treat each other with respect and care. Do not let us say hurtful things toward each other. Don't let us judge others by their skin, race, family, friends, or anything else. Everyone deserves a chance to be themselves and to act how they wish to act. It is unfair to judge others. We do not wish to be judged, so we should not be judgmental either. Help those who judge others to stop and realize the mistake they are making, so they may give that person a chance. Amen.

Kelly
Academy of the Holy Names
Albany, NY

Adonai Shalom
"Lord of Peace"

Shalom Adonai
Lord, let there be peace in my heart,
so that it may be open to feel love,
kindness, and goodness.

Shalom Adonai
Lord, let there be peace in my life,
so that I can listen to and learn from others
who seem so different from me.

Shalom Adonai
Lord, may I have the opportunity to create
a peaceful environment with
lifestyles that include all my neighbors.

Shalom Adonai
Lord, please grant me peace,
that I may find contentment in your world,
so that "nation shall not lift up sword against nation,
neither shall they learn war any more" (Isaiah 2:4).

Marisa T. Garfinkel
Saint Thomas More Academy
Magnolia, DE

Rejoice with those who rejoice, weep with those who weep. Live in
harmony with one another; do not be haughty; . . . do not claim
to be wiser than you are. Do not repay anyone evil for evil, but take
thought for what is noble in the sight of all.
                    (Romans 12:15–17)

God, we are so often caught up
In the hustle and bustle of our daily lives
That we forget there is a world outside of our own,
A world where people live on the margins of life
And have problems much more serious than our own.

Help us to take up our cross, Lord,
To have compassion for those who suffer
And to bear the responsibility of eliminating violence, hunger,
    and homelessness from our world.
Help us always to remember that they are not just "those people,"
They are our brothers and sisters in Jesus Christ,
And in them he dwells among us.

God, we alone cannot bring peace and happiness to our world.
To try would lead only to failure and despair.
Help us to realize that only by your grace and strength
Can we truly undertake the great enterprise that is your will.
Let your love fill our lives so that we may live every day
Knowing that we have truly given our best.
Amen.

Jaris C. McClain
Bishop McNamara High School
Forestville, MD

God, you have given me all I need to be content. I have a loving family, caring parents, entertaining siblings, a good heart, an intelligent mind, and a respectful disposition. You have given me these things out of love—unselfish, undying love. Help me to remember your love when I am troubled and when I am scared. I have all I need by having faith. Thank you for faith, and thank you for nonmaterial gifts.

And religion does make life rich by making us content with what we have. We didn't bring anything into this world, and we won't take anything with us when we leave. So we should be satisfied just to have food and clothing. People who want to be rich fall into all sorts of foolish and harmful desires that drag them down and destroy them. "The love of money is the root of all kinds of evil, and in their eagerness to be rich some have wandered away from the faith and pierced themselves with many pains" (1 Timothy 6:10).

Susan Schott
Roncalli High School
Indianapolis, IN

Love your neighbor as yourself.

(Matthew 19:19)

Dear God,
This world is full of prejudice and discrimination.
Help us to love one another,
Help us to understand each other's feelings,
Help us to have the courage to stand up for what is right.
Amen.

Matthew Norris
Our Lady of Perpetual Help
Ellicott City, MD

God, help me to do good
    when everyone else does bad.
God, help me to be fair
    when everyone is biased.
God, help me to care
    when everyone does not.
God, help me to see the way
    when everyone is blinded.
God, help me to be truthful
    when everyone lies.
God, help me to live with love in my life
    when everyone is filled with hate.
I ask you for these things because you are
    "the way, and the truth, and the life" (John 14:6).

Giovanni Jovanovic
Lake Michigan Catholic High School
Saint Joseph, MI

O God, help us to become better people
and to understand others in their time of need.
At this age we do not know much,
and hurt others by not knowing.
Help us to become more open and kind to others.
Let us not mock people for being different,
but instead admire that special quality.
Give us the courage to do what is right,
and also to forgive and to show mercy.
"Blessed are the merciful,
for they will receive mercy" (Matthew 5:7).
Amen.

Bao Kim Nguyen
Aquinas High School
La Crosse, WI

"All who exalt themselves will be humbled, but all who humble them-
selves will be exalted," Jesus said (Luke 18:14).
This is one of the best pieces of advice that he ever gave us.
Too many people in this world lack humility
because society places too much value on wealth and ability.
Trying to do tasks better than the rest
makes everyone get too caught up in being the best.
For God will only administer scorn
to those who always toot their own horn.
Those people who consistently brag
and make those around them want to gag.
Those who only talk about how great they are
and live in a huge house and drive a fancy car.
These people flaunt all they possess
and frown upon those of us who have less.
If they would only take the time to look, they would find
the true value of a person is in the heart and the mind.

Jacquelyn Ryan
Stella Maris High School
Rockaway Park, NY

God, help me to be humble.
Help me to not ridicule others when they fumble.

Keep me from exalting myself.
I should not place myself high up on a shelf.

God, help me to not snub others.
Help me to treat them equally because we are all brothers.

Help me to realize that I am not always right.
Let me realize this without a fight.

Help me to see when I am wrong.
Even when this is hard, help me to be strong.

Help me to recognize my sins.
"God, be merciful to me, a sinner!" (Luke 18:13).

Nicole Kelcz
Stella Maris High School
Rockaway Park, NY

Then the LORD said to Noah, "Go into the ark, you and all your household, for I have seen that you alone are righteous before me in this generation. . . . And Noah did all that the LORD had commanded him.

(Genesis 7:1–5)

This is one of my favorite Scripture passages because it says that God does have plans for all of us. It also tells us that we cannot just forget our faith like the people on Earth did back at that time.

O God, we pray that we all remember to keep you in our everyday lives. We also pray that when we sin, we are strong enough to ask for your forgiveness. We pray that we may use Noah as an example and always try to do the right thing. Amen.

Scott Jacobson
Archbishop Spalding High School
Severn, MD

Jesus said, . . . "You will not always have me [with you]."
(Mark 14:6–7)

Christmas vacation starts tomorrow.
And there is still all of this sorrow:
People fighting in the halls.
Forget about people going to the malls.
There are arguments over decorations.
Some people have no hesitations.
Does anyone know what time of year this is?
I sit and stare.
What is in the air?
Is it only me.
When will they see
that Jesus is being born?
Jesus brought us here,
so there is no need to fear.
Why should we care what others think or say,
after all, Jesus is the only one we have to impress.
He is the one who knows us best!
Christmas vacation starts tomorrow.

S. D.
Our Lady of Mount Carmel High School
Baltimore, MD

To be first you must try your hardest. You don't have to be the best, but there must be love in your heart. To be first you must make your path bright and warm, and no shadows should be found on it. To be first you need to remember your enemies as well as your neighbors. As you go through your life spreading happiness everywhere, you know that you will be first. Those who push and rush, brag and hurt others to be first "will be last, and the last"—those who are of service and compassion—"will be first" (Matthew 19:30).

Kate Sheehan
Our Lady of Perpetual Help
Ellicott City, MD

We love because he first loved us. Those who say, "I love God," and hate their brothers or sisters, are liars; for those who do not love a brother or sister whom they have seen, cannot love God whom they have not seen.

(1 John 4:19–20)

God, let me stay open-minded
For all of my days
Help me to stay clearheaded
To your all-loving ways
Show my mind how to be free
As free as a bird
Help me to stay focused
On your son's blessed word
Let me respect all
That may pass me by
Allow me to be intelligent
Till I'm with you in the sky
Keep my eyes focused
On the good of your son
Allow me to respect all
That live under the sun
Unbiased God, let me be true
Let me be right
To all you have given
Every creature in sight

Ian Noonan
Coyle and Cassidy High School
Taunton, MA

Dear God:
"What are human beings that you are mindful of them,
    mortals that you care for them?" (Psalm 8:4).
You're always in my head,
From morning until I go to bed.
I take a look at people and think,
A lot of people need a shrink.
I have no clue what they need,
Hard-core gangstas on the corner smoking weed,
When they could use the money to plant a seed,
Watch it grow and start to lead.
Not many people understand gangstas;
Not many people understand prankstas.
I know you understand them all,
Because you're the greatest from big to small.

Weston Insley
Our Lady of Mount Carmel High School
Baltimore, MD

No one has ever seen God; if we love one another, God lives in us, and
his love is perfected in us.

(1 John 4:12)

My God, my heavenly inspiration, make me an image of your love.
Help me unveil love as you did when you died on the cross and rose
    from the dead.
When sadness invades a person's soul, let me be the light they are
    searching for.
And when the outcasts come to my door,
    let me be the shelter of hope they have longed for.
God, creator of love, give me the strength and courage to be the
    peacemaker that your people are waiting for.
Amen.

Suzanne LaBella
John Carroll High School
Fort Pierce, FL

The coming of the lawless one is apparent in the working of . . . every kind of wicked deception for those who are perishing, because they refused to love the truth and so be saved.

(2 Thessalonians 2:9–10)

As I sit, God,
along the banks of this great river of life,
I wonder . . .
How are we to guide our children,
when we see through eyes of hate?
How can we be one with the Creator,
when we are taught to segregate?
This midsummer breeze
has turned a midnight chill.
The ground beneath my feet once solid,
is now a pool of quicksand.
Our faces, blank faces,
shadows cast upon a wall of stone.
Our eyes are lit dimly,
in the reflection of the shining sun;
still we are blind.
Our tongues speak with lingual unity,
yet we are mute.
Our ears can hear a newborn babe's cry,
yet we are deaf.
Where is peace on Earth?
God, bring us peace.
We ask you with bowed heads
and humble hearts,
guide our hands with the
gentleness of your love.
Guide our feet with righteousness
so that we may continue our journey
home to you, our God.
Creator of the universe, heal these wounds
of earthly sin and disbelief.

Give us the courage to praise your holy name
when we are faced with the forces of evil.
Our day will come, God,
when we dance on the rays of the sun,
hand in hand,
reunited with our sisters and brothers.
Out of this human darkness,
will emerge a holy light.
We wait.
We pray.
Come now, our God.

Amanda Lee Exum
Saint Gregory High School
Chicago, IL

Oh, my God, help me go through life,
through the moments of happiness and bliss,
as well as the times of pain and heartache.
Help me to be tolerant.
"Happy are those who find wisdom,
     and those who get understanding" (Proverbs 3:13).
Happiness exists in erasing our stereotypes
and judging not by appearances or rumors.
I need your guidance to truly be wise
and to truly be tolerant.
Guide me and I will learn.
Amen.

Neha Ohri
Coyle and Cassidy High School
Taunton, MA

Teach me your way, O LORD,
    that I may walk in your truth.

(Psalm 86:11)

In this beautiful world, filled with battle and rage,
In the wealthy countries where its children are starving,
In oceans where pollution destroys God's creatures,
In cities where our brothers and sisters are homeless,
In towns where mothers kill their children,
In homes where a family is broken out of selfishness,
In this troubled time, God, help us choose to follow your lead.
Let us know how our anger and frustration has torn our world.
And let us see truth in a world of darkness.
Amen.

Christina Enoch
Maryvale Preparatory School
Brooklandville, MD

In the Bible, Matthew 7:1–2 says: "Do not judge, so that you may not be judged. For with the judgment you make you will be judged, and the measure you give will be the measure you get." God, please help me to not judge people before I even know them. And help people to not do the same to me. I also am asking you to please keep the world free from hatred within religious, sexual, racial, and cultural issues. Please do this, God, and the world will be a much better and more peaceful place for all of us to live in. Also, with the peace that you preserve, many lives will be saved. Please watch over us all forever with your greatest strength.

Jason Hughes
Christian Brothers Academy
Albany, NY

God, sometimes it's hard to do what I must do;
Sometimes I feel too tired,
Sometimes I feel too sad,
Sometimes I feel too bad,
Sometimes it's just too much.
The other day I read the Proverbs:
"The craving of the lazy person is fatal,
    for lazy hands refuse to labor.
All day long the wicked covet,
    But the righteous give and do not hold back" (21:25–26).
Sometimes I get off track, God.
I think of how I will benefit from things.
But maybe, God, sometimes I should try.
I should do what I must do
Because others need me to.
Sometimes.

Aloni Prince
Bishop McNamara High School
Forestville, MD

Life. What is life? Most of us walk around not really knowing what we are here for. All that we do know is that we are special because God has put us on this great earth. We question God by wondering what good one person could do. Then we realize that a person can make a huge difference in the lives of people around him or her by following what Christ has taught us, "Love one another as I have loved you" (John 15:12). By trusting in God and this important teaching, we can make life more enjoyable for ourselves and others.

Brian Fitzgerald and Mario A. Lupone
Xavier High School
Middletown, CT

Dear Savior,
As the rain falls against my windowpane,
pieces of bark and fallen leaves brush against the gray sidewalk.
And I can see you, God; the sun is luminescent.
Peeking through the angelic clouds, you watch.
The reeds and stems of life tumble and fall backward.
But why haven't you shown us your light?
The meek and humble cry at night, bearing their wounds.
Chipped teeth and chapped hands reach for other hands,
but are left to stand in the cold—unnoticed.
They keep their eyes locked down, embarrassed.
But why haven't you shown us your light?
Many young teens who are trying to grow in your garden are stopped,
    stifled by demons.
These attack and suck their soul.
These substances lock the door to our destined path.
Why do we listen to those who want to distract us?
Please, God, why haven't you shown us your light?
The corrupted society jolts us to join them.
They hiss and stretch for our shoulders;
praying for us to be their prey.
Why haven't you shown us your light?
Young women lose their balance,
and search for their false treasures.
They are led to believe in false love and cannot reach,
but instead are shackled down.
They grow seeds in their tortured bodies and then make decisions:
"Should I keep this life or should I leave it behind?"
Then only do their eyes well up,
for knowing they cannot enter our world,
and their salted tears fall against my windowpane.
God, why haven't you shone your light upon these searching souls?
"For to this end we toil and struggle,
because we have our hope set on the living God,
who is the Savior of all people,
especially of those who believe" (1 Timothy 4:10).
Amen.

Neena Dass
Rosary High School
Fullerton, CA

Dear God,
Please help me to understand you better. In a time when everything
is attributed to science, make me a stronger believer. Help me to deal
with the troubles of our day and with how I can be a kinder, more
understanding person. Help me to help the less fortunate in society
instead of brushing them off and leaving them for somebody else to
help. Help me to see heaven as a true and imminent reality, and help
me to strive toward that goal. Last of all, help me to grow as a Christian outside of my community, and help me to find Jesus in my own
life. "Give to everyone who begs from you, and do not refuse anyone
who wants to borrow from you" (Matthew 5:42).

Lawrence Edwards
Bishop Manogue Catholic High School
Reno, NV

I say to you, Love your enemies and pray for those who persecute you,
so that you may be children of your Father in heaven; for he makes his
sun rise on the evil and on the good.
                    (Matthew 5:44–45)

God,
Let me show kindness to those who are mean to me. Let me help
others who are in need, no matter what my feelings are about them,
because often those people who are mean have experienced meanness
themselves. I know those who suffer need my help, even if they appear
difficult on the surface.

God, help me realize that there is good in every person, although
some people hide it well behind masks of hatred and toughness. The
way to experience their inner goodness is by showing respect to them.
Jesus tells us we should love our neighbors, good and bad, and particu-
larly our enemies.

For those of us who follow Jesus' teachings, showing *everyone* the
same kindness and respect strips away their masks and opens their
hearts to respect us. We ask this through Christ our Lord. Amen.

Mark Lehman
Jesuit High School
Carmichael, CA

So many people in the world are so quick to blame.
They always think they know it all,
and they always know what to say.
They do all they're asked but feel cheated by some
who never do any work, yet they get the job done.
"You were a harsh man,
reaping where you did not sow" (Matthew 25:24),
they say in vain.
But who are they to judge?
Who are they that have a right to complain?
Who are they to hide their talents in spite?
What do they gain if they save?
Help us not to be foolish and not to be spiteful,
but to give it our all, the best effort at all times.
For little things matter a lot,
even if others take the easy way out.
Let us live for ourselves and love one another,
for we are only cheating ourselves
when we keep our potential from others,
and we are judged by our own words and deeds
and not by the actions of others.

Meghan Moquin
Stella Maris High School
Rockaway Park, NY

I know how I am supposed to act,
    but sometimes it seems so hard.
When one of my friends is sick,
    I should stop and visit, or even send a card.
If the snow has blocked the doorway
    of my next-door neighbor's house,
I should go over with my shovel
    as quiet as a mouse.

I should do it because I want to,
    never expect pay.
You said, "You know the way
    to the place where I am going" (John 14:4).
This is the path
    that I choose.
This way I know
    I can't possibly lose.
I know I can
    make it through the day.
After all, I saw
    your loving way.

Melissa A. Deja
Lake Michigan Catholic High School
Saint Joseph, MI

I give you a new commandment, that you love one another. Just as I
have loved you, you also should love one another.
(John 13:34)

Dear God,
Help us to be a little loving each day.
Help us to mean what we say when we pray.
Help us to love more and to be considerate of others.
Help us to grow and grow from one another.

Make us a disciple of your Word.
Make us love and cherish the earth.
Make us not so concerned to please us.
Make us instead learn to love Jesus.

Twaun
Mercy Cross High School
Biloxi, MS

Sometimes we're afraid of what is different,
but differences shouldn't stop us from loving.
By looking deep into our hearts, we can find the courage,
the courage to overcome prejudices that exist in the world.
We can learn to accept others for who they are.
We can be a shoulder to cry on or a friend to laugh with.
We can heal and soothe with a warm embrace.
People enjoy being loved and need to know
that love will always be there no matter what.
When we feel that we have no one else,
we can know that God is always there,
always loving, forgiving, and welcoming us,
just as the father accepted the prodigal son for who he was.
Despite his sins, there was a celebration upon his return.
"This son of mine was dead and is alive again;
he was lost and is found!" (Luke 15:24).

Rita Tolan
Stella Maris High School
Rockaway Park, NY

You shall not murder.

(Exodus 20:13)

My dear God, you say we shall not kill.
But how do I forgive someone who has killed?
My world now feels tampered with.
The rocks I stood on now tremble.
The pride I had stored in me now weakens.
The trust that was instilled in me now is rotten.
I shall not kill, but who allows that man to kill?
Who allows that man to rob me of a loved one?
Who gave him permission to take what he had no ownership over?
My dear Lord God, you say we shall not kill;
yet only some listen to your words.

This is the world that promises me the land of freedom
so that I may breathe,
so that my offspring will be able to succeed.
Yes, my dear God, I shall not kill.
But in reality there still remains
that same man who will kill again, again, and again! Amen.

Tammy Alexis Smith
Saint Raymond Academy
Bronx, NY

The LORD is just in all his ways,
and kind in all his doings.
(Psalm 145:17)

I know this is true, God,
and so do most people my age.
Why then, God, are we compelled
to do the exact opposite?
We long to see your face,
yet we act as though we don't.
Why is it considered different
to be nice and to help others,
but okay to be cold and uncaring?
Please aid those who are only nice
because it makes them look good
to learn to really care.
Kind God, help all of your children
to become more just.

Rebecca Girsch
Peoria Notre Dame High School
Peoria, IL

I walked with George the other day,
And this is what he had to say:
"If this is what its come to, then
I'm glad that I've passed on.
For the foundation laid so long ago
apparently is gone.
What nation kills its future!?
This bloodshed they call a choice,
they passed this law in Satan's den,
these children had no voice!
I'll now return from whence I came
this place to never see again.
For we who tried to make things just
were of the thought In God We Trust."

Abe Lincoln wept so silently as we
looked out onto the open sea.
And when his tear-streaked face did turn
to me, he asked, "Was nothing learned?
Dred Scott called them nonpersons too;
the law was evil, wrong, untrue!
The price we paid for that grievous error
was a blood-soaked land filled with terror.
The dread now fills me to the core
for my beloved land, now Satan's whore.
For those who kill the ones most pure,
his wrath will come, of this I'm sure.
Turn now from this shadowed land
where once they held their Father's hand.
For the freedoms that we fought for
exist no more within this place
when you sanction murder of the defenseless in our race."

The redwoods stood before us;
their beauty touched the skies.
As Roosevelt struggled up from his chair,
a silk hankie dabbed his eyes.
"It's hard for me to understand this
evil in your midst.
Have freedoms been so distorted that
all reasoning has been eclipsed?
You see it was not so much the Japanese
or Hitler that we fought;
rather their beliefs within our world
and the evil that they wrought.
But this—this slaughter they call a choice—
have people tread so far
from the one we looked to,
the one born beneath the magi's star?
With foreboding in my very soul, I now
must turn away
from this Sodom and Gomorrah that's
been raised within your day."

"For the great day of their wrath has come,
and who is able to stand?" (Revelation 6:17).
This became the unanswered question
as I stood alone upon the land.
And though I see the reality
of how far we've tread from thee,
I take solace in your beloved son
And his infinite mercy.

Joselle M. Kohler
Towson Catholic High School
Towson, MD

I want to talk about suicide and pressures that teens really do have on their shoulders. High school is a difficult time for most teenagers. It's a time when we have to worry about peer pressure, sports, our appearance, and most especially our grades if we want to get into a good college. Everybody has a lot of pressure put on them, even adults. For example, my great-grandfather had to get a serious operation a few years ago. He did get it, and everything seemed to be fine, but actually it wasn't. He was so used to being able to walk around and fix things that he came to a point when he felt he was a burden on my family. He committed suicide. Even in the Bible, when Abraham had problems, he was always constant in his faith in God and never gave up: "The LORD will provide" (Genesis 22:14).

When my grandfather committed suicide, it was the hardest situation that ever happened to my family. Now I'm sure most teens have considered suicide, but when you think it takes your troubles away, it honestly doesn't. Not only does it hurt your friends, but it has a horrible lasting effect on your family. So I'm asking anyone that is even considering taking their own life, please don't—it's not worth it. Pray, get help, and trust that God and people will bring you hope.

Courtney Furlong
Allentown Central Catholic High School
Allentown, PA

Talking with God

I have loved you with an everlasting love;
    therefore I have continued my faithfulness to you.
                            (Jeremiah 31:3)

I see your pain and I want to help you,
But you don't see me.
My heart cries out loud for you,
But you can't hear it.
I give you sweet words of wisdom,
But you won't taste them.
I send you imperishable flowers of hope,
But you can't smell them.
My love for you is the greatest,
But you don't feel it.
You want to know where I am?
Look around, and you'll see;
I am right here.
Communicate to me everything;
I am listening.
Now, with an open soul, heed me;
I will renew you.
Trust in me;
I know everything and more.
Love me;
I will always love you.

Cathy Campion
Little Flower Catholic High School for Girls
Philadelphia, PA

Discipline always seems painful rather than pleasant at the time, but later it yields the peaceful fruit of righteousness to those who have been trained by it.

(Hebrews 12:11)

God, watch over me
during my times of difficulty.
When I call, come to me,
and you shall have my love indefinitely.
When my enemies attack me, be my shield.
When I thirst for violence, be the yield
to rid the sin and make me healed,
so that my eyes see your kingdom revealed.

And when it seems like all is wrong,
be the hope that I long
to see and hear in the song
of your presence that seems to be gone.
And when I don't understand your ways,
help me to live in the good old days,
and I will listen to all that you say
and never think of going astray.

When I am sick and feeling bad,
give me the strength that I never had.
When I want money to make me glad,
give me your love, to keep me from being sad.
And when someone I care about passes above,
send down your Spirit, the holy dove,
to remind me that they are just one of
the many who will live eternally in your love.

Andy Kim
Our Lady of Mount Carmel High School
Baltimore, MD

God is our refuge and strength,
a very present help in trouble.

(Psalm 46:1)

When I see darkness,
help me be your light.
When I see sadness,
bring gladness to sight.
When there is tiredness and despair,
let your strength be there.
When there is no laughter,
bring sweet peace to the soul.
When there is no life,
let your Spirit make us whole.
When there is no love,
let your love fill my heart.
When I am lonely,
let your presence console my loneliness.
When there is no tomorrow
and night fills the air,
thank you, God,
I know you are there!

Latoya N. Mahaffey
Notre Dame High School for Girls
Chicago, IL

Dear God,
Every once in a while, I see a beautiful sunset, a bird with brilliant colors, or maybe even the peaceful flow of a river. And when I see these things, I know that something so beautiful must come from you. If eternity is all of your works in perfection, then I can't wait to see endless sunsets, millions of colorful birds, and to be surrounded by the peaceful flow of rivers. "There is no speech, nor are there words; their voice is not heard; yet their voice goes out through all the earth" (Psalm 19:3–4).

Mary T. Grady
Saint Thomas More Academy
Magnolia, DE

When you pass through the waters, I will be with you;
    and through the rivers, they shall not overwhelm you;
when you walk through fire you shall not be burned.
                                                            (Isaiah 43:2)

God, I need your help in many different ways
Even though I'm a disobedient sheep who tends to go astray
I desire your love and forgiveness when I turn against your will
And I need you beside me when my journey is all uphill
Please open my eyes when I need some insight
And when my pathway darkens, shine upon it your light
When I stumble and fall, take me under your wing
Rehabilitate me and show me how to do the right thing
If I'm on the "good path" yet trouble finds me there
Take my hand, carry me, wrap me in your love and care
God, I know you love me because you allowed my birth
So all I ask is that you protect me as I walk your earth

Alanna Simmons
Our Lady of Mount Carmel High School
Baltimore, MD

The times of my life when I am feeling blue,
The only one I can call on is you.
I close my eyes and say in my heart,
"The LORD is my shepherd, I shall not want" (Psalm 23:1).
You never try to judge or show any hate
As you see all my tears and my heartaches.
You give me the will to try again each day.
Just thinking of your goodness makes me happy.
You fill me with your spirit by showing me that I should
Always be nice to others and always do good.
With all these words, my Lord, I just wanted you to see
How through my heart I write a personal prayer from me.

Jasmin Karima Porter
West Philadelphia Catholic High School
Philadelphia, PA

God,
Sometimes I find life so overwhelming. I may feel that no one cares about me and no one is listening. But when I find myself down, all I have to do is look up. After all, you, God Almighty, are watching over me every hour of every day. If I feel like I cannot overcome the obstacles that are in front of me, all I have to do is remember that I can and will do all things through Christ who strengthens me. God, you are truly the answer to all my prayers! "I can do all things through [Christ] who strengthens me" (Philippians 4:13).

Heidi

Our Lady Star of the Sea Church

Port Isabel, TX

If the world hates you, be aware that it hated me before it hated you.
(John 15:18)

Loving God,
Just because I disagree a lot, it seems like the world is angry with me.
And I notice that when I'm down, the world ignores me.
Why do I sometimes make bad decisions and upset those I love?
Why do I sometimes clam up
    and give the silent treatment to my friends?
Why do I sometimes feel that everyone ignores me?
Why do I feel alone?
When I do something sinful, would you help me ask for forgiveness?
When I close off those who love me,
    would you help me to reach out?
When I feel ignored, would you talk to me?
God, I know sometimes I ignore you and fail to follow Jesus' path, but
    please have pity on me because I am imperfect and just trying to
    survive.
I ask this through Christ, our Lord, amen.

Ian Meeks

Jesuit High School

Carmichael, CA

If my God is calling,
why is it that I cannot hear?
Be it my struggles in school,
my troubles with my family,
or am I just not listening?
For those who do not listen
fail to hear. This is me.
God, I shall do what you ask of me.
I ask for your strength and power,
for the will to hear and fulfill your commandment.
"If you only will listen to me!" (Genesis 23:13).

J. M. N.
Cathedral Preparatory School
Erie, PA

Dear God,
I could use a little guidance, and I thought you would probably be able
to help. Sometimes I find it hard to see the good in some people. The
way they dress, their hair, and sometimes their makeup makes me blind
to what is really inside them. So many people are dressing differently,
being individual, and not conforming to society. They are ones that are
looked down on. They are the ones who get turned away from because
of their appearance. I can't stand this intolerance. I don't like it at all.
It is not right. But the problem is, I find myself doing it as well. I don't
know why. I wish I could stop, but it is really hard. If you could just help
me out a little. Maybe open my eyes? Maybe guide me the right way,
so maybe I won't be so judging of others? Give me the strength to
remember what you said through Paul to the Ephesians: "There is one
body and one Spirit, just as you were called to the one hope, . . . one
Lord, one faith, . . . one God and Father of all" (Ephesians 4:4–6).
Help me to realize God is in everyone. Thanks a lot for reading my
letter. Hope to hear from you soon.
Signed,
Truly Sorry

Rebecca Horn
Holy Trinity Parish
Columbia, PA

For [God] will hide me in his shelter
    in the day of trouble;
he will conceal me under the cover of his tent;
    he will set me high on a rock.
Now my head is lifted up
above my enemies all around me.

(Psalm 27:5–6)

God, during times of distress, shelter me with your love and courage.
Show me I have nothing to fear, for all is good in God.
Help me rise above evil and remain there.
Prove that prayer for an enemy is more potent
than actions against my foes.

Katie E. Woodruff
Immaculata Academy
Hamburg, NY

I am the vine, you are the branches. Those who abide in me and I in
them bear much fruit, because apart from me you can do nothing.

(John 15:5)

Dear God,
I'll ask this many times,
I'll ask this over and over again.
Will you be there to pick me up when I fall down;
will you dry my tears when I am crying;
will you be my friend when I am lonely;
will you be my strength when I am weak;
will you walk beside me when I am troubled?
You are my vine and I am your branch,
and without you I can do nothing.
Branches grow from vines, and therefore I grow from you.

Jizelle A. Ramos
Aquinas High School
Bronx, NY

Everyone then who hears these words of mine and acts on them will be like a wise man who built his house on rock. . . . Everyone who hears these words of mine and does not act on them will be like a foolish man who built his house on sand.

(Matthew 7:24–26)

God, sometimes it is difficult to be like the sensible man. I know what my parents, family, and church have taught me. But just like the rain and torrents that plague the house, so the rain and torrents of the world beat against me. It is so difficult to be sensible sometimes. But your word has told me that I should put my faith in you.

When my peers encourage me to do things that I know I shouldn't, I have to look where my house is built. Is it on the rock or in the sand? Who is more important, them or you? While I always try to make you more important, I know that there are times when I slip too. I guess my head is stuck in the sand. Maybe I just need the rain to wash the sand out of the cobwebs of my brain. There I will find you.

Help me to always build upon that rock, which is you, and to keep my house and treasure within your care. Amen.

Sean A. Logan
Peoria Notre Dame High School
Peoria, IL

When I sit in darkness,
    the LORD will be a light to me.

(Micah 7:8)

God, no matter how bad things get, you are there to guide us, whether or not we realize it. You are a good friend whom we can always turn to. You illuminate the path to happiness. We turn to you and not the cheap answers of society.

God, be our guide and walk beside us. Light our path so that we do not wander off the road. Where there is confusion, show us the way, and where there is doubt, heal our ignorance. For this and our intentions, help us, God. Amen.

Pete Gleason
Archbishop Spalding High School
Severn, MD

Then I acknowledged my sin to you,
    and I did not hide my iniquity;
I said, "I will confess my transgressions to the LORD,"
    and you forgave the guilt of my sin.

(Psalm 32:5)

Dear God:
When I thought you would shame me, you loved me.
When I thought you wouldn't understand, you understood.
When I felt I couldn't go on, you carried me.
When I turned away from you, you guided me right back to you.
When I was scared and confused, you assured me.
When I was burdened by sorrow, you took the load away.
When the world turned it's back on me, you were there.
When I sinned I felt shame, and thought you would disown me;
I thought you would leave me, but you never stopped loving me.

Chenel Montgomery c/o "OO"
Notre Dame High School for Girls
Chicago, IL

Dear God,
It seems as if I'm constantly questioning my own abilities. I'm afraid of not meeting the expectations of others and those of my own. How do I become strong?

Teach me how to become a capable person who is ready and willing to face every situation. No matter how hard the task or the time it takes to be done, give me the courage to overcome anything, the same strength and courage you gave your son, so I may emerge a better person with more love for myself, others, and above all, a greater love for you.

"The wicked flee when no one pursues, but the righteous are as bold as a lion" (Proverbs 28:1).

Breanne Marie Murphy
Bishop Manogue Catholic High School
Reno, NV

I will seek the lost, and I will bring back the strayed, and I will bind up
the injured, and I will strengthen the weak.

(Ezekiel 34:16)

God, the almighty, I'm scared, worried, and in pain.
I am concerned about others, but mainly with myself.
Give me the strength to believe that you will always be at my side.
When you say, "I will bind up the injured,
and I will strengthen the weak,"
is it true?
Will you always make me feel better
and guide me through the many dark paths of life?
Do you really love and help us individually,
even with the many children you have?
Is it wrong to question you?
Please, God, give me courage and guidance.
But most of all, God, give me love, support, and protect me.
I will always believe in you and seek you
to fill the emptiness in my heart.
I love you!

Cathy Rodriguez
Aquinas High School
Bronx, NY

God, you called Samuel in the night. He recognized it was you and
said, "Speak, for your servant is listening" (1 Samuel 3:10). Please help
me to realize that you are calling me, and help me to respond with just
as much faith as Samuel did. Help me to realize that you are calling me
to serve you through the little things I encounter every day. Teach me to
listen more carefully for your call.

Laura Teta
Villa Maria Academy
Malvern, PA

Relieve the troubles of my heart,
    and bring me out of my distress.

(Psalm 25:17)

Jesus, friend,
Do you remember when you were a teen?
When you were mocked and treated mean?
When "everyone was doing it" and you couldn't?
When everyone sinned and you wouldn't?
We face these things every day,
and we're so confused in every way.
Our parents yell, our teachers command.
It's hard to follow the ten rules you demand.
A broken friendship can cause us stress.
Sometimes our lives are such a mess.
Please help us get through this phase,
because without your love we're in a daze.
We'll live our moments before they're gone,
and see you in heaven before too long.

Jennifer K. Buranich
Mount Mercy Academy
Buffalo, NY

Our God is a God of salvation,
    and to GOD, the Lord, belongs escape from death.

(Psalm 68:20)

Dear God,
Carry us along your path, and guide us into your good works. Keep us strong and faithful to carry the goodness of all creation. Bring us to you so that we may be with you the rest of time. Be with us day by day, God, and carry us through our tough times so that we will turn back to you. Amen.

Steve Turner
Peoria Notre Dame High School
Peoria, IL

Let everyone who hears say, "Come."
And let everyone who is thirsty come.
(Revelation 22:17)

Holy Friend,
We all thirst for reason in our chaotic lives. We all hunger for meaning.
Let us stop our frenzied search and realize that we need to look no
more. For you, God, are always there waiting for us to accept you into
our lives so that you might make us a part of your eternal one. For
those who deny their need for you, let them see how their life lacks
your gift. In our hardships, let us not forget how you brought us in and
quenched our needs, so that we will not turn our backs on your love.
Amen.

Kevin
Christian Brothers Academy
Syracuse, NY

My eyes waste away because of grief;
    they grow weak because of all my foes.
(Psalm 6:7)

Dear God,
I pray for myself as well as my peers as we face the struggles, heart-
breaks, and friendships of another year, another age, another generation. I pray for the needs of others as well as myself as we step into the
era: the age of high school. Help me to understand my feelings, my
strengths, and my weaknesses. Help me to put together the pieces of
my puzzle as I step closer to college. To pull myself further out of an
experience and to push toward a whole new experience, I must defi-
nitely pray to you for help, especially in the near future. Amen.

Courtney C. Cahill
Saint Gertrude High School
Richmond, VA

Do not worry about how you are to speak or what you are to say; for what you are to say will be given to you at that time.
(Matthew 10:19)

Life is filled with ups and downs, happy times and bad times.
Having faith in God doesn't mean that life will always be easy.
We will still have the good times and the bad times,
but there will be a difference if we have faith.
God wants to help our faith grow stronger and
knocks at the door of our heart.
Will we open the door?

Brandy Witner
Muskegon Catholic Central High School
Muskegon, MI

In Matthew 4:7, Jesus says, "Do not put the Lord your God to the test." I often find myself praying in times of need rather than in times of thanks. I often find myself saying, "Jesus, if you truly love me . . ." I have realized that I am constantly putting you, God, to the test by saying, "If there really is a God . . ." Maybe I should consider taking out the "ifs" and putting in "I know" so my statement could read, "Jesus I know you truly love me, could you please help me get through this day with a positive attitude." Amen.

Natalie R. Doiron
Vandebilt Catholic High School
Houma, LA

God, it seems like I spend all my time waiting, whether in line or for an answer from you. Teach me how to wait and remain patient. Calm my anxious thoughts and desires, and help me to know that you always know what is best for me. Whenever I feel anxious or impatient, remind me, "Great is [God's] steadfast love toward us, and the faithfulness of the LORD endures forever" (Psalm 117:2).

Loria Walthall
John Carroll Catholic High School
Birmingham, AL

Dear God,
My mind is filled with worries,
My heart is scared to love.
My body shakes with fear,
My soul cries out for help.
You say,
"Do not let your hearts be troubled" (John 14:1).
My heart is the center of me.
So by not letting my heart be troubled,
I'm free!
Free to love and follow you,
And though I do not know
What my future will be,
I am sure that I'll be rewarded
By the happiness of others and
My opportunity to be with you.

Caitlin Cullitan
Lake Michigan Catholic High School
Saint Joseph, MI

Teach me your way, O LORD,
    that I may walk in your truth;
    give me an undivided heart to revere your name.
                    (Psalm 86:11)

God, when I am wrong, show me the right path.
Teach me to trust in your word and follow the way to happiness.
Let me make mistakes so I can learn from them
    and come back to you.
Understand me, God, and direct my life in a way that I can follow.
When I am questioning your existence, show me that you are real.
Trust that I will come back to you, my God, when I know the truth.
Let me believe and praise your name.

Kathleen Beers
Saint Gertrude High School
Richmond, VA

One does not live by bread alone,
but by every word that comes from the mouth of God.
(Matthew 4:4)

Please help me, God.
Help me overcome distractions and be a stronger person.
I know how much I mean to you.
I know that jewelry, food, and clothes
are not the only things you offer.
May these things not distract me.
Give me power to overcome my need for them.
Please help me realize that your faith in and love of me
is what helps me get through the day.
I know that every word you say, I will not understand.
But I will follow your commands and be a good disciple.
I know that without you I would be lost and not find my way.
Now, God, I know that we live
by every word coming from your mouth.
I will follow you in the journey
and won't let anything keep me from you.
Amen.

Elenid Acosta
Saint Raymond Academy
Bronx, NY

To you, O LORD, I lift up my soul.
O my God, in you I trust.
(Psalm 25:1)

Help me through every day and guide me in my actions. Help me to do
your will so that I may serve you to the best of my abilities. I lay my soul
in your hands so that you can do what you want with it. Amen.

Mark Baird
Loyola Blakefield High School
Towson, MD

The clever see danger and hide;
   but the simple go on, and suffer for it.
                                    (Proverbs 22:3)

God, please grant me solid vision so that I may see what is ahead of me. Bless me with the sense to avoid all meaningless obstacles that I may create for myself. Grant me these things so that the path I have already traveled will not be filled with regret. Clear my vision and straighten my path so that I may be blessed with your vision as I travel toward you.

Tim Burke
Towson Catholic High School
Towson, MD

Be strong and courageous; do not be frightened or dismayed, for the LORD your God is with you wherever you go.
                                    (Joshua 1:9)

Dear God,
I know that you are always with me, but sometimes it is hard for me to know what you are calling me to do. Help me to always listen to your word, both in the Scriptures and in the Mass. Guide me in making important and difficult decisions in my life. Thank you for blessing me with so many gifts; please help me to know how and when to use them.

   Whenever I am discouraged or afraid, I know that I can always turn to you in prayer. Please help me to remember that you should be the main focus in my life. Sometimes I find it difficult to keep you as the most important part of my life. It is easy for me to get caught up in the less important things in life. I am working very hard to keep you as the most important part of my life, because without you I would be nothing.

E. Mengers
Villa Maria Academy
Malvern, PA

God, help me when I am in distress,
when I am having a bad day and feel like a mess.
Help me face each day one at a time,
so I can have a chance to shine.
"Be a rock of refuge for me" (Psalm 31:2).
Help me get to heaven and be with you eternally.
God, I need your help, I am nothing without you.
Also help my friends, because they need your help too.

Joseph Barnitz
Brother Martin High School
New Orleans, LA

Lord, everything I do should be centered around you. It says in the Bible, "Commit your work to the LORD, and your plans will be established" (Proverbs 16:3). Sometimes it may seem hard to include you in the things I do in my daily life. Help me to remember all things you did for us and are doing for us now, so that everything I do will display your importance in my life. Amen.

S. J. L.
Aquinas High School
La Crosse, WI

God of life,
Often we are so blinded by the tears of defeat and deafened by the roar of success, we are unable to see or hear you. So we walk aimlessly through life. "Redeem me from human oppression, that I may keep your precepts" (Psalm 119:134). Help us to slow down, to stop, to open our eyes, ears, and hearts so that we might be able to recognize your presence in our lives. Amen.

Paul Mikio Kavanaugh
Xavier High School
Middletown, CT

God, I am sorry for worshiping materialistic objects instead of focusing on you. I am sorry for forgetting that through you, only, can I experience true joy: "For all people who were ignorant of God were foolish by nature; and they were unable from the good things that are seen to know the one who exists, nor did they recognize the artisan while paying heed to his works" (Wisdom of Solomon 13:1). Please, God, help me focus on you, the creator of all things. Help me to recognize you in my everyday life.

Ryan Manger
Brother Martin High School
New Orleans, LA

Why, O LORD, do you stand far off?

(Psalm 10:1)

Why, Lord, do you stand at a distance and pay no attention to these troubled times? Sometimes I feel as though you punish us on purpose. Help me to be more patient with you. Nothing should ever come between us. It is too easy to forget my morals and blame you for mistakes. I get so caught up in little things that seem so important instead of getting caught up in you. Don't let troubles become the center of my life. Let me always remember that you always will be what is most important. I now forget my troubles and offer this prayer to you.

Brigid J. Bush
Aquinas High School
La Crosse, WI

 I believe; help my unbelief!

(Mark 9:24)

Dear God,
I know that it is hard to believe in miracles, but I know that you will open my eyes and show me how. Sometimes I don't understand why things happen. Maybe there's a certain reason for why they happen, but I can't find it. Please help me to believe in the truth about things I cannot understand. Please help me to find reality when I don't know where it is. Look for me when I'm lost and need your help because sometimes my faith is not strong enough and I need someone to guide me.

Ashley M. Burch
Holy Spirit Parish
McAllen, TX

Index by School

Academia María Reina
San Juan, PR
    Claudia Calderón-Pacheco   53
    Natalia Canto   45

Academy of Mount Saint Ursula
Bronx, NY
    Shaniqua V. Lyles   31

Academy of the Holy Names
Albany, NY
    Michelle Emma   32
    Kelly   69
    Jamie Vanessa Woodall   28

Allentown Central Catholic High School
Allentown, PA
    Courtney Furlong   90

Aquinas High School
Bronx, NY
    Jizelle A. Ramos   97
    Cathy Rodriguez   100

Aquinas High School
La Crosse, WI
    Adam Binsfeld   53
    Brigid J. Bush   108
    Kristen Jungen   41
    S. J. L.   107
    Bao Kim Nguyen   73

Archbishop Spalding High School
Severn, MD
    Pete Gleason   98
    Scott Jacobson   74

Bishop Hendricken High School
Warwick, RI
    Andrew Catauro   65
    Ben Zyons   16

Bishop Manogue Catholic High School
Reno, NV
    C. B.   13
    Sarah Binger   16
    Lawrence Edwards   83
    Nicholas Hill   55
    Breanne Marie Murphy   99
    K. S.   25
    Katherine Wieland   14

Bishop McNamara High School
Forestville, MD
    Carley   24
    J. L. H.   67
    Keenon James   39
    Kymberly Lathrop   31
    E. E. M.   38
    Mary Frances Mayo   48
    Jaris C. McClain   70
    Aloni Prince   81

Brother Martin High School
New Orleans, LA
    Joseph Barnitz   107
    Ryan Mange   108
    Eric J. Pitre   68
    Corey M. Price   67

Cathedral Preparatory School
Erie, PA
    J. M. N.   96

Catholic Central High School
Springfield, OH
Angela Fisher 37
Pamela S. Marsh 34

Catholic High School of Baltimore
Baltimore, MD
Constance Barbara David 36
Michelle Kreafle 56
Amanda Renée Smith 47
Ann Thomas 29

Christian Brothers Academy
Albany, NY
Jason Hughes 80

Christian Brothers Academy
Syracuse, NY
T. K. K. 63
Kevin 102
Susanna 20

Coyle and Cassidy High School
Taunton, MA
Mike Caputo 45
Jim Crowley 52
Patrick 47
Shawn Morales 57
Ian Noonan 76
Neha Ohri 79

Divine Child High School
Dearborn, MI
Susan Giza 52

Elder High School
Cincinnati, OH
Eric M. Tepe 20
Tim Trainor 10

Gabriel Richard High School
Riverview, MI
Jeanne 44

Holy Spirit Parish
McAllen, TX
Ashley M. Burch 109

Holy Trinity Parish
Columbia, PA
Rebecca Horn 96

Holy Trinity Student Chapel
Ypsilanti, MI
Emily Schrag 40

Immaculata Academy
Hamburg, NY
Shannon Shaw 53
Katie E. Woodruff 97

Jesuit High School
Carmichael, CA
Brian Daniel Burris 42
Jake Deterding 52
Mark Lehman 83
Ian Meeks 95
Niclas Murk 55

John Carroll Catholic High School
Birmingham, AL
Lara Obert 38
Gregory Ross Sanders 37
Loria Walthall 103

John Carroll High School
Fort Pierce, FL
Stephanie Ann LaBella 58
Suzanne LaBella 77

Lake Michigan Catholic High School
Saint Joseph, MI
Caitlin Cullitan 104
Melissa A. Deja 84
Susan Rae Janiszewski 61
Giovanni Jovanovic 72
Carrie Smietanka 50

Little Flower Catholic High School for Girls
Philadelphia, PA
Katie Boccuti 23
Cathy Campion 91

Longwood Academy
Chicago, IL
Ngonzi Crushshon 43

Loyola Blakefield High School
Towson, MD
    Mark Baird   105
    Michael Lawrence   21

Maryvale Preparatory School
Brooklandville, MD
    Christina Enoch   80

McGill-Toolen High School
Mobile, AL
    C. L. C.   17

Mercy Cross High School
Biloxi, MS
    Jarah Rider   27
    Twaun   85

Mercy High School
Middletown, CT
    Christina Tracey Czap   46
    Kim Miazga   62
    Beth Salonia   58

Mother Theodore Guerin High School
River Grove, IL
    Genesha Gutierrez   21

Mount Mercy Academy
Buffalo, NY
    Jennifer K. Buranich   101
    Jaclyn Chentfant   60

Muskegon Catholic Central High School
Muskegon, MI
    David Grillo   66
    Brandy Witner   103

Northeast Catholic High School
Philadelphia, PA
    Christopher Miley   57

Notre Dame High School for Girls
Chicago, IL
    Leilani   18
    Latoya N. Mahaffey   93
    Chenel Montgomery c/o "OO"
99

Adriana Rodriguez   54
Jenny Torres   35

Our Lady of Mount Carmel High School
Baltimore, MD
    S. D.   75
    Weston Insley   77
    Andy Kim   92
    Alanna Simmons   94
    Alison Thomas   26

Our Lady of Perpetual Help
Ellicott City, MD
    Chris Hildreth   15
    Laura Leviski   13
    Tara McDonnell   40
    Matthew Norris   72
    Kate Sheehan   75

Our Lady Star of the Sea Church
Port Isabel, TX
    Heidi   95
    Erin M. Keelin   41

Peoria Notre Dame High School
Peoria, IL
    Rebecca Girsch   87
    Sean A. Logan   98
    Matt   62
    Joseph Sullivan   59
    Steve Turner   101

Roncalli High School
Indianapolis, IN
    Jenna Hayes   49
    Gretchen Schmaltz   15
    Susan Schott   71
    Ingrid Torres   68

Rosary High School
Fullerton, CA
    Neena Dass   82
    Andraya Eisenman   32
    Jackie Schrader   63

Saint Augustine Academy
Lakewood, OH
    Mary-Frances Auner   12

Saint Gertrude High School
Richmond, VA
    Kathleen Beers   104
    Courtney C. Cahill   102
    Sarah Cannon   10
    Katie Nelson   56
    Brie Whitmire   51

Saint Gregory High School
Chicago, IL
    Amanda Lee Exum   78

Saint John the Baptist High School
West Islip, NY
    Jennifer Caban   50
    Jean Gismervik   18, back cover
    Jamie Lynn Press   60

Saint Joseph Parish
Black River Falls, WI
    Amy A. Andraska   44
    Tim Johnson   46

Saint Patrick Church
Troy, OH
    M. E. G.   49

Saint Raymond Academy
Bronx, NY
    Elenid Acosta   105
    Jessica Crystal Roman   64
    Tammy Alexis Smith   86

Saint Thomas More Academy
Magnolia, DE
    Alexis Diana Marie Christiansen   12
    Marisa T. Garfinkel   70
    Mary T. Grady   93
    Kathryn Lessard   48
    Litty Smelter   24

Saint Xavier High School
Louisville, KY
    Michael Zurkuhlen   19

Stella Maris High School
Rockaway Park, NY
    Khadija Goding   69

Dawn Harrison   42
Nicole Kelcz   74
Meghan Moquin   84
Jacquelyn Ryan   73
Rita Tolan   86

Towson Catholic High School
Towson, MD
    Tim Burke   106
    Jon Eddinger   51
    Joselle M. Kohler   88
    Kia Taylor   29

University of San Diego High School
San Diego, CA
    Dan Leake   22

Vandebilt Catholic High School
Houma, LA
    Natalie R. Doiron   103

Villa Maria Academy
Buffalo, NY
    Nga Tran   26

Villa Maria Academy
Malvern, PA
    Liz George   33
    E. Mengers   106
    Laura Teta   100

West Philadelphia Catholic High School
Philadelphia, PA
    Shantell C. Griffin   9
    L. K.   59
    Akeisha King   28
    Jasmin Karima Porter   94
    Tiffany Turner   30

Xavier High School
Middletown, CT
    Brian Fitzgerald   81
    Paul Mikio Kavanaugh   107
    Mario A. Lupone   81
    Jeff Miazga   35
    Mark S. Wooding   35